The Unforeseen Wilderness

Gene Meatyard

Wendell Berry

The Unforeseen Wilderness

An Essay on Kentucky's
Red River Gorge

TEXT BY WENDELL BERRY

PHOTOGRAPHS BY GENE MEATYARD

1971 LEXINGTON The University Press of Kentucky

Standard Book Number:
8131–1244–3

Library of Congress Catalog
Card Number: 72–147851

The authors wish to express their
gratitude to the Kentucky Research
Foundation for a grant; and to the editors
of Audubon, The Southern Review, The
Hudson Review, *and the Louisville*
Courier-Journal, *in which portions of this*
book first appeared.

A statewide cooperative scholarly publish-
ing agency serving Berea College, Centre
College of Kentucky, Eastern Kentucky
University, Kentucky State College,
Morehead State University, Murray State
University, University of Kentucky,
University of Louisville, and Western
Kentucky University.

Editorial and Sales Offices:
Lexington, Kentucky 40506

Contents

CHAPTER ONE

A Country of Edges

It is a country of overtowering edges. Again and again, walking down from the wooded ridge tops above the Red River Gorge one comes into the sound of water falling—the steady pouring and spattering of a tiny stream that has reached its grand occasion. And then one arrives at a great shady scoop in the cliff where the trail bends and steps and skids down to the foot of the fall. One looks up twenty or thirty or fifty or more feet to where the water leaps off the rock lip, catching the sunlight as it falls. Maybe there will be a rainbow in the spray. The trail may have passed through little shelves or terraces covered with wild iris in bloom. Or along the streamsides below the falls there may be pink lady's slippers. The slopes will be thickly shrubbed with rhododendron, darkened by the heavy green shade of hemlocks. And always on the wet faces of the rock there will be liverwort and meadow rue and mosses and ferns.

These places are as fresh, and they stay as fresh in the memory, as a clear, cold drink of water. They have a way of making me thirsty, whether I need a drink or not, and I like to hunt out a pool among the rocks and drink. The water is clear and clean and cold. It is what water ought to be, for here one gets it "high and original," uncorrupted by any scientific miracle. There will be a clean gravelly bottom to the pool and its edges will bear the delicate garden-growth of the wet woods. There are the enclosing sounds of the water falling, and the voices of the phoebes and the Carolina wrens that nest in the sheltered places of the cliffs. Looking and listening are as important as tasting. One drinks in the sense of being in a good place. There is such a quenching as can never be had from a pump or a faucet.

> *Here are your waters and your watering place.*
> *Drink and be whole again beyond confusion.*

Those lines of Robert Frost live very near to the experience and the knowledge of such places. For this drinking is an attempt at some ceremony of atonement and communion, and it suggests the inadequacy of our culture. In a place of such purity and beauty, free to men along with the other creatures, but not manmade and beyond the powers and the understanding of men, what is there to do but perform some gesture of humility and gratitude before the mystery of creation? But we have no saying or ceremony that is appropriate. It is the modern muteness and paralysis. Such religion as we have had has aimed us strictly Heavenward; along with our exploitive economic values, it has prepared us to voyage to the moon and into space, not to be fully and humanly at home in the rocky dells of the Red River Gorge.

The critical fact about water, wherever you find it in the Red River Gorge, is motion. Moving, it is gathering. All the little seeps and trickles of the slopes, the tiny streams heading

2

up near the ridgetops and leaping and tumbling down the steep ravines—all are moving toward their union in the river.

And in the movement of its waters the place also is in motion; not to the human eye, nor to the collective vision of human history, but within the long gaze of geologic time the Gorge is moving within itself, deepening, changing the outline of its slopes; the river is growing into it like a great tree, steadily lengthening its branches into the land. For however gentle it may appear at certain seasons, this network of water known in sum as the Red River moves in its rocky notches as abrasive as a file.

How the river works as maker of the landscape, sculptor, arm of creation will probably always remain to some degree speculative, for it works with immeasurable leisure and patience, and often it works in turmoil. Although its processes may be hypothesized very convincingly, every vantage point of the country is also a point of speculation, a point of departure from the present surface into the shadowy questions of origin and of process.

By what complex interaction of flowing water, of weather, of growth and decay was that cliff given its shape? Where did this house-sized boulder fall from, what manner of sledging and breaking did it do coming down, what effect has it had on the course of the stream? What is actually happening now in all the swirling rapids and falls and eddies and pools of the river in flood? We know the results. But because we have not a thousand years to sit and patiently watch, because our perspective is not that of birds or fish or of the lichens on the cliff face but only of men, because the life of the Gorge has larger boundaries than the life of a man, we know very little of the actual processes.

To come to any understanding of the Red River one must acquire a sense of how minute and manifold are its workings, how far beyond count are its lives and aspects and manifestations. But one must also sense its great power and its vastness. One must see in it the motive force of a huge landscape, the formal energy of all the country that drains into it. And one must stand on its banks and consider that its life and meaning are not merely local, but that it is intricately involved in all life and all meaning. It belongs to a family of rivers whose gathering will finally bring its water to mingle with the waters of the Yellowstone and the Kanahwa and the ocean. Its life belongs within—is dependent upon and to some extent necessary to— the life of this planet.

And so in the aspect of the river, in any of its moods, there is always a residual mystery. In its being it is too small and too large, too complex and too monumentally simple, too powerful and too delicate, too transient and too ancient and durable ever to be comprehended within the limits of a human life. One looks at the face of the water as at the night sky, knowledge serving but to lead the mind into mystery.

On the last Saturday in March we set out from Fletcher Ridge to walk down Mariba Fork, Laurel Fork, and Gladie Creek to the river. Last weekend there was deep snow. This
morning it is sunny and warm. We walk past an old house site

on the ridge—the clearing now grown up in thicket, the ground still covered with the dooryard periwinkles—and then down a steep path through the cliffs. As we approach the stream at the foot of the slope we begin to find hepaticas in bloom. They are everywhere, standing up in bright jaunty clumps like Sunday bouquets beneath the big poplars and beeches and hemlocks, and on the tops of boulders.

The path fades out. We follow the rocky edges of the stream, descending with the water gradually deeper into the land. As along all the streams of the Gorge, the country is divided by stones or cliffs or trees into distinct enclosures, a series of rooms, each one different in light and looks and feeling from all the rest.

We find other flowers in bloom: trout lilies, rue anemones, trailing arbutus with its delicately scented blossoms almost hidden among the dead leaves. But running through all that day like an insistent, endlessly varied theme in a piece of music are the little gardens of hepaticas. Climbing onto a streamside terrace or entering the mouth of a ravine, we find the ground suddenly rich with them, the flowers a deep blue or lavender or pink or white. They are like Easter gone wild and hiding in the woods.

Downstream from where we camp that night we can see the rocky point of a cliff, high up, with a dead tree standing alone on it. And at twilight a pair of pileated woodpeckers cast off from that tree and make a long steep descent into the woods below, their flight powerful and somehow abandoned, joyous, accepting of the night.

Our walk ends the next day in the midst of a violent down- 5 pour. We know that, behind us, the country we have passed through is changing. Its maker has returned to it yet again to do new work.

Flowing muddy and full, frothing over its rapids, its great sound filling the valley to the brim, the river is inscrutable and forbidding. The mind turns away from it, craving dry land like a frightened swimmer. The river will not stay still to be regarded or thought about. Its events are too much part of the flow, melting rapidly into one another, drawn on by the singular demand of the current.

Other times when the river is low, idling in its pools, its mysteries become inviting. One's thoughts eagerly leave solid ground then and take to the water. The current has ceased to be a threat and become an invitation. The thought of a boat comes to mind unasked and makes itself at home.

At such a time, a bright morning in early June, a canoe seems as satisfying and liberating as a pair of wings. One is empowered to pass beyond the shore, to follow the current that, other times, standing on the shore, one has merely wished to follow.

We wake at dawn, camped high on one of the ridges. Below us the hollows are drifted deep in white mist. While we eat breakfast and pack up we watch the mist shift with the stirrings of the air, rising, thickening and then thinning out, opening here and there so that we can see through to the treetops below, and closing again. It is as if the whole landscape is moving with a gentle dreaming motion. And then we drive down the windings of Highway 715, through the rapidly thinning mist, to the river. And now our canoe lies on the water in the shade-dappled weak light of the early morning. We have the day and the river before us.

Through the morning we paddle or drift through the long pools, idling with the river, stopping to look wherever our curiosity is tempted. We see a kingfisher, a water thrush, a Kentucky warbler, a muskrat, a snake asleep on an old tire caught on a snag, a lot of big, fat tadpoles three or four inches long, dragonflies with brilliant green bodies and black wings. In the clear shoals we see fish, and at intervals we pass the camps of fishermen, places their minds will turn back to, homesick, out of the confinement of winter and city and job. These places are usually quiet and deserted. We have already passed the fishermen, fishing from the top of a boulder upstream, or we will find them in a boat a little way below.

On the bar at the mouth of Wolfpen Creek, where we stop for lunch, we watch several black and yellow swallowtail butterflies drinking together on a spot of damp sand. They are like a bouquet of flowers which occasionally fly away and return again.

Where the swift clear water of Wolfpen enters the river a school of minnows is feeding. They work up the current over a little shoal of rippled sand, and then release themselves into the flow, drifting down through the quick water shadows to start again.

And all along the stream are boulders as big as houses that have broken from the cliffs and tumbled down. They are splotched with gray lichens and with mosses and liverworts; where enough dirt has collected in cracks and depressions in the stone there will be clumps of ferns or meadow rue or little 7 patches of bluets. Above the high water line, where the current cannot sweep them, the long drama of soil-building has taken place on the tops of some of these rocks, so that they are now covered with plants and trees, and their surfaces look much like the surrounding forest floor. Those within reach of the floods are cleaner and more stony looking. They are not to be imperceptibly eaten away by the acids of the decay of vegetation and by the prizing of root and frost; they are being hewed out like sculptures by the direct violence of the river. Those that stand in the stream have been undercut by the steady abrasion of the current so that they rise out of the water like mushrooms. Going by them, one thinks of the thousands of miles of water that have flowed past them, and of the generations of boatmen, Indians and white men, that have paddled around them or stopped to fish in their shadows—and one feels their great weight and their silence and endurance. In the slanting light of the early morning the reflections off the water waver and flicker along their sides, the light moving over them with the movement of water.

There is no river more intimate with its banks. Everywhere the shore rises up steeply from the water like a page offered to be read. Water-borne, one seems always within arm's reach of the land. One has a walker's intimacy with the animals and plants of the shore as well as a boatman's intimacy with the life of the water. Without rising from one's seat in the canoe one looks into the mossy cup of a phoebe's nest fastened to the rock and sees the five white eggs.

At intervals through the day we tense and focus ourselves as the river does, and move down into the head of a rapid. We pass through carefully, no longer paddling as we wish but as we must, following the main current as it bends through the rocks and the grassy shoals. And then we enter the quiet water of the pool below. Ahead of us a leaf falls from high up in a long gentle fall. In the water its reflection rises perfectly to meet it.

CHAPTER TWO *The One-Inch Journey*

The mollusk-shell of civilization, in which we more and more
completely enclose ourselves, is lined on the inside with a
nacreous layer that is opaque, rainbow-tinted, and an inch
thick. It is impossible to see through it to the world; it works,
rather, as a reflecting surface upon which we cast the self-
flattering outlines and the optimistic tints of our preconceptions
of what the world is.

These obscuring preconceptions were once superstitious
or religious. Now they are mechanical. The figure representative
of the earlier era was that of the otherworldly man who thought
and said much more about where he would go when he died
than about where he was living. Now we have the figure of
the tourist-photographer who, one gathers, will never know
where he is, but only, looking at his pictures, where he *was*.
Between his eye and the world is interposed the mechanism
of the camera—and also, perhaps, the mechanism of economics:
having bought the camera, he has to keep using it to get his
money's worth. For him the camera will never work as an
instrument of perception or discovery. Looking through it, he
is not likely to see anything that will surprise or delight or
frighten him, or change his sense of things. As he uses it, the   *11*

camera is in bondage to the self-oriented assumptions that thrive within the social enclosure. It is an extension of his living room in which his pictures will finally be shown. And if you think the aspect or the atmosphere of his living room might be changed somewhat by the pictures of foreign places and wonders that he has visited, then look, won't you, at the pictures themselves. He has photographed only what he has been prepared to see by other people's photographs. He has gone religiously and taken a picture of what he saw pictured in the travel brochures before he left home. He has photographed scenes that he could have bought on postcards or prepared slides at the nearest drug store, the major difference being the frequent appearance in his photographs of himself, or his wife and kids. He poses the members of his household on the brink of a canyon that the wind and water have been carving at for sixty million years as if there were an absolute equality between them, as if there were no precipice for the body and no abyss for the mind. And before he leaves he adds to the view his empty film cartons and the ruins of his picnic. He is blinded by the device by which he has sought to preserve his vision. He has, in effect, been no place and seen nothing; the awesomest wonders rest against his walls, deprived of mystery and immensity, reduced to his comprehension and his size, affirmative of his assumptions, as tame and predictable as a shelf of whatnots.

Throughout their history here, most white men have moved across the North American continent following the fictive coordinates of their own self-affirming assumptions. They have followed maps, memories, dreams, plans, hopes, schemes, greeds. Seldom have they looked beyond the enclosure of preconception and desire to see where they were; and the few who have looked beyond have seldom been changed by what they saw. Blind to where they were, it was inevitable that they should become the destroyers of what was there.

One of the oldest and most persistent legends of the white man's occupation of Kentucky is that of John Swift's silver. Swift was a silver miner who is supposed to have wandered in the Kentucky mountains in about 1760. He left a journal describing his adventures, paramount among which was the discovery of a marvelously rich lode of silver. The journal contained directions for finding this wealth and also a map, but because of Swift's poor knowledge of the country and its land-marks both directions and map have proved meaningless.

And that very meaninglessness has assured the survival and the dispersal of the legend, and of the indefatigable dream that the legend represents. Today, according to Thomas D. Clark, there are still people in the Kentucky mountains "who had rather seek fortune by searching for nebulous silver than by plowing corn." And that region is said to be littered with vaguely defined sites where *maybe* John Swift found and then lost his silver mine. One of those places is the Red River Gorge, and a tributary of the Red is named in commemoration of Swift's passage through that country: Swift Camp Creek.

There could be no better parable of the white man's entrance into Kentucky. For John Swift is the true forefather of our history here, and his progeny have been numerous. They have descended upon this land from the eastward passes and from their mothers' wombs with their minds set on the dream of quick riches to be had, if not from a vein of precious metal, then from coal or from logs. Or from the land itself, for those who preferred to plow rather than hunt silver have all too often followed the agricultural method known as "mining," by which the growth is taken from the land and nothing given back, until the fields are exhausted like a mined-out seam of coal.

The wealth of a place is not to be reckoned by its market value at some given moment. Its real wealth is not just its present value, but its *potential* value as it continues through time; and therefore its wealth is not finally reckonable at all, for we do not know how long the world, or our species, will last.

I have heard strip miners justify the destruction of large tracts of the earth by figures showing that the value of the mineral lying under the ground was greater than the value of the crops or the forest then standing on the surface. They would be right if the world, or if people's dependence on it, should come to an end the day after the seam was mined out.

It is certainly possible that the world or the human race may come to an end pretty soon. But another possibility—and a much more demanding possibility, too—is that the human race may continue for thousands of years. We can't possibly say how many thousands it may be. But in Asia there are agricultural lands that, by wise farming methods, have been kept continuously productive of food crops for six thousand years. If the people of China and Korea and Japan have depended on their farmlands for six thousand years, we in America might reasonably prepare to be dependent for at least that long *14* on ours. And so before we accept the arguments of the strip miners, we should ask other experts to compute for us the value of the produce of the soil overlying the coal seams for a period of six thousand years, and we should weigh that value against the value of the mineral.

When a mineral deposit is mined out, the miners are done with that place forever. When a logging crew has cut the marketable trees from a boundary of timber, it may be that a generation or more will pass before another logging crew will return. But the farmer's relation to a place, and his dependence on it, are continuous, and because of that he is the figure who most accurately represents what our relation to the earth is. And Americans who contemplate the history and the behavior of the American farmer are not apt to find him the source of much comfort. There have been, and continue to be, noble exceptions; nevertheless, the historical *tendencies* that I am talking about seem to me clearly established.

Characteristically, the American farmer, moving into new lands to the west, did not subject himself to the disciplines and restraints implicit in the nature and the topography of the new land. Instead, he pretty much ignored where he was and went about his business on the assumption that the place he had come to was the same as the place he had come from. Thus the Englishman, starting as a farmer in Virginia, was obeying not so much a vision of what a farm in Virginia might or ought to be, as a memory of what farming in England *was*. And the son of a Virginia farmer, opening a farm in the Kentucky wilderness, imitated the Virginian's imitation of an Englishman. Because of differences in soil and climate and rainfall this

15

imitativeness has been, in general, a failure. On relatively flat lands the performance of the American farmer has often enough been poor. On steep lands his performance has been almost invariably disastrous. Kentucky farmers have often destroyed whole hillsides in only a few crop years. In some of the levelest lands they have done more damage in a generation than the thoroughly indigenous Japanese farmers did to their land in six millennia. And the Kentucky farmer, going west, over-grazed the plains—largely, I believe, on the assumption that the grass grew there the same way he had seen it growing in Kentucky.

But the American farmer has not been so destructive just because of an illusion as to his whereabouts. For years, almost from the beginning, there has been in this country a social fashion that has led people to believe that life in the city is better than life in the country, that there is something de-grading in any work that dirties the hands, that work of any kind has its highest meaning and reward in leisure. Many of our farmers, because of these attitudes, have come to look upon farming not as an honorable calling or as a meaningful way of life, but as a form of bondage. Consequently, the aim and the ideal of their labor has not been a wise and preserving use of the land, but escape, both from the land and from the work it requires. And so the farmers have often farmed their land not in accordance with a vision of what it is or what it ought to be, but in accordance with a dream of where they would like to go as soon as they can get the money. It is these who have "mined" the land, for to build the fertility of a field, putting back as well as taking away, is to cut the margin of immediate

profit; that would be to make a long-term investment in the

future of the land, and their only thought of the future is the wish that as much of it as possible will be spent somewhere else. Their hopes and dreams lying elsewhere, they can have no clear and disciplining sense of where they are, and so the old destructive ways persist. They are institutionalized, in fact, in the efficiencies and chemical shortcuts of "agri-business."

Several months ago I watched a farmer prepare the ground and plant and grow a crop of corn on a ridge draining into the North Fork of the Red River. The ridge was narrow, falling off steeply on both sides like a barn roof. It was not suited to row-cropping at all. My guess was that, like a great deal of steep Kentucky land, it had been logged off years ago, and then cropped and pastured until the land would no longer sustain a profitable growth, and then abandoned. A growth of trees and bushes had covered it again. And then, having learned nothing from experience, and perhaps driven by the adverse markets that have nearly always afflicted farmers—and farmlands— in America, this man had returned to it, to practice on it yet again the "new ground" methods of his grandfathers, cutting and burning all the bushes and trees, plowing between the stumps, and planting corn. The crop was puny, hardly worth the man's trouble and labor, much less the damage to the ridge. The erosion, beginning as soon as he uncovered the ground, will continue—and he will thus continue to invest in his crop—long after his earnings from it have been spent and forgotten.

A practice of the same vintage and wisdom is that of over-grazing such slopes. The assumption is that the only function of grass is to serve as feed for livestock, and so the stock is permitted to graze it to the root. The result, again, is the ero- *17*

sion of the slopes and the steady depletion not only of the watershed but of the pasture. The result is the siltation and flooding
of the streams. The result is the impoverishment and degrada-
tion and displacement of the people. For the reasons I have
mentioned, and doubtless for other reasons that I don't know,
the obvious lesson has never been learned: You can't uncover
steep land without destroying it.

And the causes of these ruinous attitudes and practices
are by no means coextensive with the ridges and hollows of the
Red River country. They have their origin in our life and history
as a people here in America. They have their origin in our
failure to this day to be able to assign any value other than
economic to the land, and to the life of and on the land, and to
men's labor—and in our complacent assumption that our
economy will somehow turn out to be the same as nature's,
that it somehow has something to do with the truth about our
life in this world. Of all illusory enclosures that of the American
economy is the narrowest and the worst. To be blind to
everything outside the competence of a bank clerk is, as we
have been told over and over, to be spiritually dead; it is also,
as we are slowly learning, to be an accomplice in the death of
the world. It is a form of insanity. But even in economic terms it
has failed to make sense. In the intelligence of a man governed
exclusively or mainly by economic concerns there appears to
be an inclination, compelling as the law of gravity, toward the
quickest profit. Cutting a stand of timber, he is apt to diminish
the possibility that more timber will ever grow. Opening a
strip mine, he takes out the coal, and assures in the process
that there will be no more produce from that land for genera-
18 tions, perhaps forever. Overpasturing a hillside this year, he

reduces the number of cattle he will be able to pasture next year. And so he is not only spiritually dead and criminally destructive, on his own terms of economics he is stupid; his "practicality" is only folly. And this man—whom our grandchildren will look upon as the incarnation of evil, if they survive the results of his folly—is the man we have most honored and entrusted with power.

When a man operates in the landscape either as a dreamer of "better" places or as a simple digit of the "economy," he is operating without moral or ecological controls. And without controls himself, he destroys the controls of nature: the layers of vegetation and topsoil that, if let alone, would cover the land and preserve it. With nothing to break the fall of the rain or to absorb and hold the water, the slopes become little more than roofs, shedding the runoff into the river. And then the river begins to be known and feared as a destroyer, and the people downstream begin to cry out for "flood control"—as if control would not exist if some human being did not invent it, and as if it were something people could cry out for and surely get.

And for this very complex problem, with its complex sources in the abused watershed and in the minds of the people, the city fathers downstream and the Army Corps of Engineers offer a stunningly simple solution: Build a dam! The downstream citizens, sealed up in their clamshell, are aware of only one phenomenon: high water. It appears to them that Nature, man's enemy, is warring against them, threatening to fill the clamshell with a muddy flood. And so the ancient battle cry is raised: Conquer nature! Nature has already been conquered on the slopes upstream, and so now it has to be conquered downstream.

The Corps of Engineers is a famous nature-conquerer, and it is always alert for that familiar battle cry. But the Corps of Engineers has its clamshell too, and when the cry is heard it feels no need to go outside, but looks instead around its rainbow-tinted walls at its charts and maps and tables and graphs and gauges showing the direction and velocity of the political wind. From the Engineers' commanding vantage point it is clear to them that what is needed is a dam. And the processes of dam making are set in motion. All this is done by the manipulation of abstractions: between two points on a topographical map a dam is to be built, requiring a certain predicted expenditure of dollars, backing the water to the level of a certain contour, able to control a certain amount of runoff from the slopes upstream and to deliver a specified number of gallons daily to the city water companies downstream. The *place* of the resulting lake does not matter, because it is not known. For the inexhaustible details and aspects and facts and mysteries of the life of the river valley there is to be substituted the abstraction of a water level tabulated upon pieces of paper. And that abstraction of mechanics attracts the most abstract of human desires—avarice. For a lake means Tourists, Recreation, Developments, Deals, Money. Thus, by what some will call human genius and others the munificence of God, an ecological disaster will be turned into an economic bonanza. Now the walls of the shell are alight with wonderful dreams; civilization is like being surrounded by a technicolor movie, and it looks like everybody's going to have plenty of ticket money.

But enter the place itself. Leave behind the theories and the propaganda, the presumptions, the charts and statistics, and go into the watershed of the Red River. Drive along the ridges where the tributaries head up, and look at the over-cropped, overpastured, denuded slopes. Look at the despoiled carcass of a land that was once bountifully forested, ecologically healthy and whole, and of incalculable economic potential. Consider the results of methods that grew out of ignorance and misunderstanding and economic constraint.

And then consider the river itself. Even now there are stretches of it that look as wild and unspoiled, you imagine, as they did a hundred years ago. That, to be sure, is something to be thankful for—but so far you are only looking at the surface. Step into the stream and wade down it for a few hundred steps. And notice that wherever the current slows you are walking, not over the clean rocky or weedy bottom of a healthy stream, but in mud. In places the mud is more than knee deep. It is the soil of the ridges and slopes upstream, the wasted flesh of a living creature that has been stricken by a lethal disease.

To a man standing in that mud, aware of what it means, the idea of the proposed "flood control dam" is a giddy fiction, a fairy tale that reduces science to the level of the crudest superstition. It is not as obviously stupid, but it is just as stupid nevertheless, as the idea of putting a stopper in the mouth of a volcano. For what the dam will be, if the misuse of the water-shed continues, is the first step in the creation of a swamp. It will have nothing to do with the control of anything, but will be only another manifestation of the lack of moral and social

21

and economic control that made the need for "flood control" in the first place. It will finally be seen to have a good deal more to do with the illusions of the short-term investment and the quick profit and the easy remedy than with any reality of the environment.

The proponents of the dam in the Red River Gorge are the most recent heirs of John Swift in that part of the country. They have been entranced, as Swift was, by the dream of ease—of easy wealth, of easy answers, of easy fulfillments. And the dream is accompanied, necessarily, by the assumption that such ease is not destructive.

It almost always *is* destructive. For the labor of preserving the life of the world, of which our lives are a part and on which they depend, is difficult and complex and endless. In nature all that grows is finally made to augment the possibility of growth, and so nothing is wasted. This year's leaves decay and enter the intricate life and process of the soil, which assures that there will be more leaves another year. It is this pattern and only this—not any that he may conceivably invent—that man must imitate and enter into if he is to live in the world without destroying it.

The task of preserving the life of the world has little to do with the present values of American society. It has almost nothing to do with our concepts of wealth and profit and success and luxury and ease. It has nothing at all to do with short-term investments, or short-term anything else. It is not recognizable to a short-term intelligence. It involves a man in work that he can neither live to finish nor imagine the end of. It is humble work, often involving the use of the hands. It requires a tolerance and respect for mystery. Its model figures are not to be found among the great figures of our history: our artists, inventors, soldiers, statesmen—but among humble people whose lives were devoted laboriously and ceremoniously and lovingly to the life of their land: tribal people and peasants.

John Swift has other heirs in the country of his legend who will no doubt be surprised and outraged to be so considered. And yet I believe that they and the dam builders, whose activities they are apt to deplore, have this ancestor in common. They are the lovers of "scenery." Now that the Red River Gorge has become famous because of the efforts to keep it from being made into a lake, the scenery lovers cause traffic jams there on the weekends. They come by carloads and busloads, following one another, bumper-to-bumper, along the narrow blacktop, stopping only at "scenic overlooks," or perhaps not stopping at all. For them the automobile has become a censoring device. They want to see only what can be seen sitting down and at highway speeds. They supposedly are charmed by the notion of a wilderness place, but they want it neatly packaged in "views"—as if the world were a commodity, to be served up to consumers like hamburgers at a drive-in. Like the tourist-photographer's camera, their eyes seek out only what resembles what they have already seen, or what resembles pictures they have seen, or what they have been told is "beautiful." They will exclaim over a long view of a monumental rock or cliff, but will never see the phoebe's nest clinging to its face. Still less will they be aware of the cycles of living **23** and dying, exuberance and pain, plenty and want, eating and being eaten, growth and decay, that course through the scene they are looking at.

The conservation movement has so far concentrated too much on scenic places. This is changing, and it can't change too soon. There will have to be a concern with agricultural methods, with city environments, with the watersheds of unspectacular streams, with the widespread preservation of farm woodlands and wetlands. To preserve only the scenic places is to invite their destruction, either in the process of the destruction of their surroundings, or by the overcrowding of people who have no other places to go.

The scenery-oriented conservationists are the ones who have introduced *esthetics* into the vocabularly of conservation, and then made nonsense of it by failing to see its relation to practicality or, for that matter, to reality—so that the term is now bandied about by publicists as if it referred to a *quantity* of something to be purchased at the buyer's convenience, and by strip miners and other ruiners as if it referred to a handy camouflage for disgrace. The concern with esthetics has been mostly a dealing with appearances, as if anything that "looks good" is all right. An example of the esthetic approach to conservation is the Kentucky law requiring junkyards to be surrounded by a high fence—which only conceals the problem and, in practice, often looks worse. Another is a proposal, once advanced by West Kentucky strip miners, that areas destroyed by strip mining should be landscaped along the main highways.

The truth, as always, is more difficult. Natural beauty is no

more than a by-product of natural health. Decently and frugally used, the earth will be beautiful; disdained, exploited and abused, it will be ugly, as well as unhealthy, and there will be no way to "beautify" it. When one relates to the world in terms of its "scenery," then one is apt to go around talking about "beautifying" such things as strip mines and slums. But what is being destroyed cannot be made beautiful. The notion that a process of ruin can be accompanied and offset by a process of beautification, that all is well if the country looks pretty from the roadside, is only another illusion of ease, like John Swift's silver. It is another technicolor pipedream to keep us ignorant and endangered—and dangerous—shut up in our shell.

There is something suicidal, and more sinister than that, in this quest for easy wealth and easy answers, for it proposes goals that are dead ends, that imagination and desire do not go beyond. Once the precious vein of silver has been found, once the speculation in land or mineral or timber has paid off, then a man's work will be over; he will have escaped forever the drudgery of the plow or the office. But if a man has destroyed in himself the capacity to enjoy work—and he does this inevitably by working toward the goal of escape from work— then how can he possibly enjoy leisure? He can't, of course. And our country is full of men who have worked and sacrificed and deferred pleasure, and as a result achieved all that they dreamed of—and who, having now neither work nor goal, are perfectly miserable. Such a life is shallow and destructive; despising the work it has undertaken out of hatred for work, it has unwittingly learned to despise itself; destroying peace and innocent pleasure in seeking for ease, it has unwittingly destroyed itself; despising and destroying itself, it helplessly despises and destroys the world.

That is the predominant form of our life now. But there is another form that life can take. We can learn about it from exceptional people of our own culture, and from other cultures less destructive than ours. I am speaking of the life of a man who knows that the world is not given by his fathers, but borrowed from his children; who has undertaken to cherish it and do it no damage, not because he is duty-bound, but because he loves the world and loves his children; whose work serves the earth he lives on and from and with, and is therefore pleasurable and meaningful and unending; whose rewards are not deferred until "retirement," but arrive daily and seasonally out of the details of the life of his place; whose goal is the continuance of the life of the world, which for a while animates and contains him, and which he knows he can never encompass with his understanding or desire.

Comparatively few white men have ever lived this way in America. And for the ones who have, or who have attempted to, it has been difficult, for the prevailing social current has always flowed away from the land, toward the city and the abstractions of wealth and specialization and power. The pressures against a modest and preserving life on the land have been manifested most immediately in adverse agricultural markets and in an overwhelming prejudice against all things identifiable as "country." These pressures have already destroyed the small farmers of most sections of the country, and are well advanced in the destruction of the rest.

Broken from the land, contemporary Americans do not now settle down in some city, as to some extent they used to, but remain migratory from job to job and from neighborhood to neighborhood and from city to city. But these wanderings have no real function. They do not spread knowledge and skills and songs as the wanderings of artists and poets once did, and they are not linked to natural cycles as were the wanderings of Arctic peoples and desert nomads. They are artificial wanderings, unappeasable searches for John Swift's silver in all its modern manifestations: more money, shorter hours, easier work, higher status.

Not only does all this moving around destroy the integrity and continuity of marriages and families, as has been often enough said, but it destroys any possibility of a disciplined relation to the earth. For it seems a fact that most minds require, as a condition of insight and discipline, some measure of continuity, and some measure of the devotion that can only associate itself with continuity. Unchecked by any feeling that they may return soon, or at all, weekenders strew the public woodlands and streamsides with trash. Lacking any association with the disciplines of maintaining the farmlands the year round, urban hunters have become notorious as destroyers of fences and gates—and as most indiscriminate shooters.

The conservation movement has become almost exclusively a matter of power struggles between agencies and corporations and *organizations* of conservationists. The agencies and corporations are motivated by visions of power and profit. The conservation organizations are motivated by principles which very largely remain abstract, since the number of people who can *know* a place is necessarily too small to protect it, and must therefore enlist the aid of people who do not know it but are willing to protect it on principle.

I should make it clear that I recognize the need for the conservation organizations, and that I am emphatically on their side. But the organizations, by themselves, are not enough. If they are to succeed in any way that is meaningful, or perhaps if they are to succeed at all, their work must be augmented by an effort to rebuild the life of our society in terms of a decent spiritual and economic connection to the land. That can't be done by organizations, but only by individuals and by families and by small informal groups. It will have to be done by leaving the cities and the suburbs and making a bond with some place, and by *living* there—doing the work the place requires, repairing the damage other men have done to it, preserving its woods, building back its fertility and its ecological health—undertaking, that is, the labor, the necessary difficulty and clumsiness of discovering, at this late date and in the most taxing of circumstances, a form of human life that is not destructive.

In the Red River Gorge there is such a family as I am talking about: people drawn out of the city to an ancestral tract of farmland enclosed in that wilderness—drawn back by loyalty and love, and by a sense, having learned the alternatives, of what such a place and such a life mean and what they might be made to mean. The house can be reached only by footpath in wet weather, and in the best of weather only by tractor. The house sits at the edge of the woods, at the foot of a great sheer cliff, overlooking the open fields of the bottomlands. The quiet of the wilderness rises over it, enormous, a silence millions of years old concentrated in the looming gray cliff face. It is a quietness that has been accepted; the house, one senses, has over the years been cleansed of all unnecessary sounds. It seems somehow to have assumed the deeply musing inwardness of the stone that towers over it. It is the dwelling place of a sorrowing intelligence that understands the crisis of the Gorge as a part of the crisis of the world. When the Gorge is flooded and this family loses its home and its history and the disciplining and reassuring sense of its place in the world, that will be no isolated incident, not one of those sacrifices that are sometimes required of individuals for the sake of the common good. It will be another small step in the spread of an epidemic, a chronic and cancerous devaluation of the life of the world and the lives of people. When this family is forced out of its home, which has been for them not just a place to sleep and eat but a loving task and a hopeful promise and a joy, they will join the thousands of the American dispossessed who have been driven out to make room for roads and airports and lakes and such like. When people can't be secure in their homes because of the demands of the public interest, then the public interest is serving us as a foul god.

What that household promises to the world is not the possibility of better organizations, but the possibility of better life. It has taken its life knowingly and lovingly from its place. And in return it offers to the place the promise of life—a longer and more abundant and better cherished life than can be offered   *29* it by any government or organization. For if the good principles of governments and organizations can't be made to live in the lives of people and places then they are dead—or, at best, five percent alive in the bungling dutifulness of functionaries.

And that household, meaningful and promising as it is, appears doomed, for it can survive only in its particularity, and it is caught between two abstractions: the organizations that would destroy the Gorge, and the organizations that would preserve it. The forces of destruction, of course, consider nothing except their dreams of profit, and the consequent methods. And the forces of preservation cannot consider or represent private claims because the Gorge cannot be saved, or damage to it limited, except as a *public* place. There is, so far as I know, no force that represents the frail possibility that security in one's home implies the right to stay in it. The Public Interest, in some of its manifestations, is another colored lantern slide on the wall of our snug clamshell—howbeit most remunerative to some of its servants. If the public is destroyed piecemeal "in its own interest"—well, that is regrettable, for the liars in public office will have to contend with a further diminishment of confidence in the government, but the Public Interest must be served. Meanwhile, who worries about a few more dispossessed families—they're getting *paid*, aren't they?

What will cure us? At this point it seems useless to outline yet another idea of a better community, or to invoke yet another anthropological model. These already abound, and we fail to make use of them for the same reason that we continue to

destroy the earth: we remain for the most part blind to our

surroundings. What the world was, or *what we have agreed that it was*, obtrudes between our sight and what the world *is*. If we do not see clearly what the nature of our place is, we destroy our place. If we don't see where we are, we are more dead than alive; if we cannot see how our own lives are drawn from the life of the world, and how they are involved and joined with that greater life, then we live in a deathly sleep, and such efforts as we may make to preserve the greater life will be inept and perhaps destructive. If like John Swift we do not know the country and its landmarks, if we are unable to see where we are in relation to it, then we lose it and lose its promised abundance. We lose our lives.

The effort to clarify our sight cannot begin in the society, but only in the eye and in the mind. It is a spiritual quest, not a political function. Each man must confront the world alone, and learn to see it for himself: "first cast out the beam out of thine own eye; and then shalt thou see clearly to cast the mote out of thy brother's eye."

And so from the figure of the silver hunter John Swift, I turn to the figure of the photographic artist—not the tourist-photographer who goes to a place, bound by his intentions and preconceptions, to record what has already been recorded and what he therefore *expects* to find, but the photographer who goes into a place in search of the real news of it.

His search is a pilgrimage, for he goes along ways he does not fully understand, in search of what he does not expect and cannot anticipate. His undertaking involves a profound humility, for he has effaced himself; he has done away with his expectations; he has ceased to make demands upon the place. He keeps only the discipline of his art that informs and sharpens *31* his vision—he keeps, that is, the practice of observation—for before a man can be a seer he must be a looker. His camera is a dark room, and he has made a dark place in his mind, exultant and fearful, by which he accepts that he does not know what he is going to see, he does not know the next picture. He has entered into the darkness—in order to see! But for the moment the dark lens holds only a vague potency, like a lentil seed, still one with the mystery of what will come next, which is one with the mystery of the wilderness and of the creation.

And then there comes a breaking of the light—and there is another shore to step out of the dark upon, lighted by a blooming flower like a candelabra. We are invited on! We are led on as by the promise of a feast spread for us that we do not yet know. In the shadows a little stream steps down over a ledge of rock into the light. Beyond are the trees, and the darkness again.

Knowing the heaviness of the dead-end search for wealth and ease, what a relief and a joy it is to consider the photographer's pilgrimage to the earth. He is seeking, not the ultimate form of the creation, for he cannot hope to find that, but rather the inexhaustible manifestations of form within the creation. Walking through the woods, he finds within the apparent clutter of trunks and branches a row of trees, leading the eye on. He sees the entrance of the sun upon a rock face. Among the dark trees, time and again, there appears suddenly a tree of light. In the early morning the mist is white and thick in the valley so that the ridgetops seem to float in the sky; looking, one's eyes receive a kinship with the eyes of a sage in the mountains of China a thousand years ago. The light withholds itself from the darkness inside the earth, and the darkness in the earth opens out to the light. The paths and streams clamber through notches in the cliffs. In the narrow ravines the water flashes over the rock lip, enters the great calm and ease of falling, descending into shadow; and the trees strain up out of the tumbled rocks into the light. In the midst of its ageless turmoil in the Roughs of the Upper Gorge, the river breaks out of the rocks, collects in an open pool, and stands still. A small stream is flowing out of the dark tunnel it has followed down through the woods, entering the greater opening of the river— and a man is standing there, not the uproarious creature of machines, but just a man standing quietly there, almost hidden by the leaves. The photographer is nowhere to be seen. These images are the record of his pilgrimage, and he has moved on. Once, these served him as landmarks, each one defining his whereabouts and leading him on to the next, and thence on again. It is an endless quest, for it is going nowhere in terms of space and time, but only drawing deeper into the presence, and into the mystery, of what is underfoot and overhead and all around. Its grace is the grace of knowing that our consciousness and the light are always arriving in the world together.

The camera is a point of reference, a bit like a compass though not nearly so predictable. It is the discipline and the opportunity of vision. In relation to the enclosure we call civilization, these pictures are not ornaments or relics, but windows and doors, enlargements of our living space, entrances into the mysterious world outside the walls, lessons in what to look for and how to see. They limit our comfort; they drain away the subtle corruption of being smug; they make us a little afraid, for they suggest always the presence of the unknown, what lies outside the picture and beyond eyesight; they suggest the possibility of the sudden accesses of delight, vision, beauty,   *33* joy that entice us to keep alive and reward us for living; they can serve as spiritual landmarks in the pilgrimage to the earth that each one of us must undertake alone.

Always in big woods when you leave familiar ground and step off alone into a new place there will be, along with the feelings of curiosity and excitement, a little nagging of dread. It is the ancient fear of the Unknown, and it is your first bond with the wilderness you are going into. What you are doing is exploring. You are undertaking the first experience, not of the place, but of yourself in that place. It is an experience of our essential loneliness, for nobody can discover the world for anybody else. It is only after we have discovered it for ourselves that it becomes a common ground and a common bond, and we cease to be alone.

And the world cannot be discovered by a journey of miles, no matter how long, but only by a spiritual journey, a journey of one inch, very arduous and humbling and joyful, by which we arrive at the ground at our feet, and learn to be at home. It is a journey we can make only by the acceptance of mystery and of mystification—by yielding to the condition that what we have expected is not there.

CHAPTER THREE *An Entrance to the Woods*

On a fine sunny afternoon at the end of September I leave my work in Lexington and drive east on I-64 and the Mountain Parkway. When I leave the Parkway at the little town of Pine Ridge I am in the watershed of the Red River in the Daniel Boone National Forest. From Pine Ridge I take Highway 715 out along the narrow ridgetops, a winding tunnel through the trees. And then I turn off on a Forest Service Road and follow it to the head of a foot trail that goes down the steep valley wall of one of the tributary creeks. I pull my car off the road and lock it, and lift on my pack.

It is nearly five o'clock when I start walking. The afternoon is brilliant and warm, absolutely still, not enough air stirring to move a leaf. There is only the steady somnolent trilling of insects, and now and again in the woods below me the cry of a pileated woodpecker. Those, and my footsteps on the path, are the only sounds.

From the dry oak woods of the ridge I pass down into the rock. The foot trails of the Red River Gorge all seek these stony notches that little streams have cut back through the cliffs. I **pass** a ledge overhanging a sheer drop of the rock, where in a wetter time there would be a waterfall. The ledge is dry and mute now, but on the face of the rock below are the characteristic mosses, ferns, liverwort, meadow rue. And here where the ravine suddenly steepens and narrows, where the shadows are long-lived and the dampness stays, the trees are different. Here are beech and hemlock and poplar, very straight and tall, reaching way up into the light. Under them are evergreen thickets of rhododendron. And wherever the dampness is there are mosses and ferns. The faces of the rock are intricately scalloped with veins of ironstone, scooped and carved by the wind.

Finally from the crease of the ravine I am following there begins to come the trickling and splashing of water. There is a great restfulness in the sounds these small streams make; they are going down as fast as they can, but their sounds seem leisurely and idle, as if produced like gemstones with the greatest patience and care.

A little later, stopping, I hear not far away the more voluble flowing of the creek. I go on down to where the trail crosses and begin to look for a camping place. The little bottoms along the creek here are thickety and weedy, probably having been kept clear and cropped or pastured not so long ago. In the more open places are little lavender asters, and the even smaller-flowered white ones that some people call beeweed or farewell-summer. And in low wet places are the richly flowered spikes of great lobelia, the blooms an intense startling blue, exquisitely shaped. I choose a place in an open thicket near the stream, and make camp.

It is a simple matter to make camp. I string up a shelter and put my air mattress and sleeping bag in it, and I am ready for the night. And supper is even simpler, for I have brought sandwiches for this first meal. In less than an hour all my chores are done. It will still be light for a good while, and I go over and sit down on a rock at the edge of the stream.

And then a heavy feeling of melancholy and lonesomeness comes over me. This does not surprise me, for I have felt it before when I have been alone at evening in wilderness places that I am not completely familiar with. But here it has a quality that I recognize as peculiar to the narrow hollows of the Red River Gorge. These are deeply shaded by the trees and by the valley walls, the sun rising on them late and setting early; they are more dark than light. And there will often be little rapids in the stream that will sound, at a certain distance, exactly like people talking. As I sit on my rock by the stream now, I could swear that there is a party of campers coming up the trail toward me, and for several minutes I stay alert, listening for them, their voices seeming to rise and fall, fade out and lift again, in happy conversation. When I finally realize that it is only a sound the creek is making, though I have not come here for company and don't want any, I am inexplicably sad.

These are haunted places, or at least it is easy to feel haunted in them, alone at nightfall. As the air darkens and the cool of the night rises, one feels the immanence of the wraiths of the ancient tribesmen who used to inhabit the rock houses of the cliffs; of the white hunters from east of the mountains; of the farmers who accepted the isolation of these nearly inaccessible valleys to crop the narrow bottoms and ridges and pasture their cattle and hogs in the woods; of the seekers of quick wealth in   *37* timber and ore. For though this is a wilderness place, it bears its part of the burden of human history. If one spends much time here and feels much liking for the place, it is hard to escape the sense of one's predecessors. If one has read of the prehistoric Indians whose flint arrowpoints and pottery and hominy holes and petroglyphs have been found here, then every rock shelter and clifty spring will suggest the presence of those dim people who have disappeared into the earth. Walking along the ridges and the stream bottoms, one will come upon the heaped stones of a chimney, or the slowly filling depression of an old cellar, or will find in the spring a japonica bush or periwinkles or a few jonquils blooming in a thicket that used to be a dooryard. Wherever the land is level enough there are abandoned fields and pastures. And nearly always there is the evidence that one follows in the steps of the loggers.

That sense of the past is probably one reason for the melancholy that I feel. But I know that there are other reasons.

One is that, though I am here in body, my mind and my nerves too are not yet altogether here. We seem to grant to our high-speed roads and our airlines the rather thoughtless assumption that people can change places as rapidly as their bodies can be transported. That, as my own experience keeps proving to me, is not true. In the middle of the afternoon I left off being busy at work, and drove through traffic to the freeway, and then for a solid hour or more I drove sixty or seventy miles an hour, hardly aware of the country I was passing through, because on the freeway one does not have to be. The landscape has been subdued so that one may drive over it at seventy miles per hour without any concession whatsoever to one's where-

abouts. One might as well be flying. Though one is in Kentucky one is not experiencing Kentucky; one is experiencing the highway, which might be in nearly any hill country east of the Mississippi.

Once off the freeway, my pace gradually slowed, as the roads became progressively more primitive, from seventy miles an hour to a walk. And now, here at my camping place, I have stopped altogether. But my mind is still keyed to seventy miles an hour. And having come here so fast, it is still busy with the work I am usually doing. Having come here by the freeway, my mind is not so fully here as it would have been if I had come by the crookeder, slower state roads; it is incalculably farther away than it would have been if I had come all the way on foot, as my earliest predecessors came. When the Indians and the first white hunters entered this country they were altogether here as soon as they arrived, for they had seen and experienced fully everything between here and their starting place, and so the transition was gradual and articulate in their consciousness. Our senses, after all, were developed to function at foot speeds; and the transition from foot travel to motor travel, in terms of evolutionary time, has been abrupt. The faster one goes, the more strain there is on the senses, the more they fail to take in, the more confusion they must tolerate or gloss over—and the longer it takes to bring the mind to a stop in the presence of anything. Though the freeway passes through the very heart of this forest, the modern motorist remains several hours' journey by foot from what is living at the edge of the right-of-way.

But I have not only come to this strangely haunted place in a short time and too fast. I have in that move made an enormous change: I have departed from my life as I am used to living it, and have come into the wilderness. It is not fear that I feel; I have learned to fear the everyday events of human history much more than I fear the everyday occurrences of the woods; in general, I would rather trust myself to the woods than to any government that I know of. I feel, instead, an uneasy awareness of severed connections, of being cut off from all familiar places and of being a stranger where I am. What is happening at home? I wonder, and I know I can't find out very easily or very soon.

Even more discomforting is a pervasive sense of unfamiliarity. In the places I am most familiar with—my house, or my garden, or even the woods near home that I have walked in for years—I am surrounded by associations; everywhere I look I am reminded of my history and my hopes; even unconsciously I am comforted by any number of proofs that my life on the earth is an established and a going thing. But I am in this hollow for the first time in my life. I see nothing that I recognize. Everything looks as it did before I came, as it will when I am gone. When I look over at my little camp I see how tentative and insignificant it is. Lying there in my bed in the dark tonight, I will be absorbed in the being of this place, invisible as a squirrel in his nest.

Uneasy as this feeling is, I know it will pass. Its passing will produce a deep pleasure in being here. And I have felt it often enough before that I have begun to understand something of what it means:

Nobody knows where I am. I don't know what is happening

to anybody else in the world. While I am here I will not speak, and will have no reason or need for speech. It is only beyond this lonesomeness for the places I have come from that I can reach the vital reality and essence of a place such as this. Turning toward this place, I confront a presence that none of my schooling and none of my usual assumptions have prepared me for: the wilderness, mostly unknowable and mostly alien, that is the universe. Perhaps the most difficult labor for my species is to accept its limits, its weakness and ignorance. But here I am. This wild place where I have camped lies within an enormous cone widening from the center of the earth out across the universe, nearly all of it a mysterious wilderness in which the power and the knowledge of men count for nothing. As long as its instruments are correct and its engines run, the airplane now flying through this great cone is safely within the human freehold; its behavior is as familiar and predictable to those concerned as the inside of a man's living room. But let its instruments or its engines fail, and at once it enters the wilderness where nothing is foreseeable. And these steep narrow hollows, these cliffs and forested ridges that lie below, are the antithesis of flight.

Wilderness is the element in which we live encased in the fragile enclosure of our civilization, as tenuously and precariously as a mollusk lives in his shell in the sea. It is a wilderness that is beautiful, dangerous, abundant, oblivious of us, mysterious, never to be conquered or controlled or second-guessed, or known more than a little. It is a wilderness that for most of us most of the time is kept out of sight, camouflaged, by the edifices and the busyness and the bothers of human society.

And so, coming here, what I have done is strip away this camouflage, the human facade that usually stands between me and the universe, and I see more clearly where I am. What I am able to ignore much of the time, but find undeniable here, is that all wildernesses are one: there is a profound joining between this wild stream deep in one of the folds of my native country and the tropical jungles, the tundras of the north, the oceans and the deserts. Alone here, among the rocks and the trees, I see that I am alone also among the stars. A stranger here, unfamiliar with my surroundings, I am aware also that I know only in the most relative of terms my whereabouts within the black reaches of the universe. And because the natural processes are here so little qualified by anything human, this fragment of the wilderness is also joined to other times; there flows over it a nonhuman time to be told by the growth and death of the forest and the wearing of the stream. I feel drawing out beyond my comprehension perspectives from which the growth and the death of a large poplar would seem as continuous and sudden as the raising and the lowering of a man's hand, from which men's history in the world, their brief clearing of the ground, will seem no more than the opening and shutting of an eye.

And so I have come here to enact—not because I want to but because, once here, I cannot help it—the loneliness and the humbleness of my kind. I must see in my flimsy shelter, pitched here for two nights, the transience of capitols and cathedrals. In growing used to being in this place, I will have to accept a humbler and a truer view of myself than I usually have.

A man enters and leaves the world naked. And it is only

naked—or nearly so—that he can enter and leave the wilderness. If he walks, that is; and if he doesn't walk it can hardly be said that he has entered. He can bring only what he can carry—the little that it takes to replace for a few hours or a few days an animal's fur and teeth and claws and functioning instincts. In comparison to the usual traveler with his dependence on machines and highways and restaurants and motels—on the economy and the government, in short—the man who walks into the wilderness is naked indeed. He leaves behind his work, his household, his duties, his comforts—even, if he comes alone, his words. He immerses himself in what he is not. It is a kind of death.

The dawn comes slow and cold. Only occasionally, somewhere along the creek or on the slopes above, a bird sings. I have not slept well, and I waken without much interest in the day. I set the camp to rights, and fix breakfast, and eat. The day is clear, and high up on the points and ridges to the west of my camp I can see the sun shining on the woods. And suddenly I am full of an ambition: I want to get up where the sun is; I want to sit still in the sun up there among the high rocks until I can feel its warmth in my bones.

I put some lunch into a little canvas bag, and start out, leaving my jacket so as not to have to carry it after the day gets warm. Without my jacket, even climbing, it is cold in the shadow of the hollow, and I have a long way to go to get to the sun. I climb the steep path up the valley wall, walking rapidly, thinking only of the sunlight above me. It is as though I have entered into a deep sympathy with those tulip poplars that   *43*

grow so straight and tall out of the shady ravines, not growing
a branch worth the name until their heads are in the sun. I am
so concentrated on the sun, so oblivious to anything else, that
when some grouse flush from the undergrowth ahead of me,
I am thunderstruck; they are already planing down into the
underbrush again before I can get my wits together and realize
what they are.

The path zigzags up the last steepness of the bluff and then
slowly levels out. For some distance it follows the backbone
of a ridge, and then where the ridge is narrowest there is a
great slab of bare rock lying full in the sun. This is what I
have been looking for. I walk out into the center of the rock
and sit, the clear warm light falling unobstructed all around.
As the sun warms me I begin to grow comfortable not
only in my clothes, but in the place and the day. No longer an
indifferent fact, the day lies before me now as a welcome adventure. And like those light-seeking poplars of the ravines,
my mind begins to branch out.

Southward, I can hear the traffic on the Mountain Parkway, a steady continuous roar—the corporate voice of twentieth-
century humanity, sustained above the transient voices of its
members. Last night, except for an occasional airplane passing over, I camped out of reach of the sounds of engines. For
long stretches of time I heard no sounds but the sounds of
the woods.

Near where I am sitting there is an inscription cut into the
rock:

A · J · SARGENT

fEB · 24 · 1903

Those letters were carved there more than sixty-six years ago. As I look around me I realize that I can see no evidence of the lapse of so much time. In every direction I can see only narrow ridges and narrow deep hollows, all covered with trees. For all that can be told from this height by looking, it might still be 1903—or, for that matter, 1803 or 1703, or 1003. Indians no doubt sat here and looked over the country as I am doing now; the visual impression is so pure and strong that I can almost imagine myself one of them. But the insistent, the overwhelming, evidence of the time of my own arrival is in what I can hear—that roar of the highway off there in the distance. In 1903 the continent was still covered by a great ocean of silence, in which the sounds of machinery were scattered at wide intervals of time and space. Here, in 1903, there were only the natural sounds of the place. On a day like this, at the end of September, there would have been only the sounds of a few faint crickets, a woodpecker now and then, now and then the wind. But today, two-thirds of a century later, the continent is covered by an ocean of engine noise, in which silences occur only sporadically and at wide intervals.

From where I am sitting in the midst of this island of wilderness, it is as though I am listening to the machine of human history—a huge flywheel building speed until finally the force of its whirling will break it in pieces, and the world with it. That is not an attractive thought, and yet I find it impossible to escape, for it has seemed to me for years now that the doings of men no longer occur within nature, but that the natural places which the human economy has so far spared now survive almost accidentally within the doings of men. This wilderness of the Red River now carries on its ancient processes *within* 45 the human climate of war and waste and confusion. And I know that that distant roar of engines, though it may *seem* only to be passing through this wilderness, is really bearing down upon it. The machine is running now with a speed that produces blindness—as to the driver of a speeding automobile the only thing stable, the only thing not a mere blur on the edge of the retina, is the automobile itself—and the blindness of a thing with power promises the destruction of what cannot be seen. That roar of the highway is the voice of the American economy; it is sounding also wherever strip mines are being cut in the steep slopes of Appalachia, and wherever cropland is being destroyed to make roads and suburbs, and wherever rivers and marshes and bays and forests are being destroyed for the sake of industry or commerce.

No. Even here where the economy of life is really an economy—where the creation is yet fully alive and continuous and self-enriching, where whatever dies enters directly into the life of the living—even here one cannot fully escape the sense of an impending human catastrophe. One cannot come here without the awareness that this is an island surrounded by the machinery and the workings of an insane greed, hungering for the world's end—that ours is a "civilization" of which the work of no builder or artist is symbol, nor the life of any good man, but rather the bulldozer, the poison spray, the hugging fire of napalm, the cloud of Hiroshima.

Though from the high vantage point of this stony ridge I see little hope that I will ever live a day as an optimist, still I

am not desperate. In fact, with the sun warming me now, and

with the whole day before me to wander in this beautiful country, I am happy. A man cannot despair if he can imagine a better life, and if he can enact something of its possibility. It is only when I am ensnarled in the meaningless ordeals and the ordeals of meaninglessness, of which our public and political life is now so productive, that I lose the awareness of alternatives, and feel the despair of having come to the dead end of possibility.

Today, as always when I am afoot in the woods, I feel the possibility, the reasonableness, the practicability of living in the world in a way that would enlarge rather than diminish the hope of life. I feel the possibility of a frugal and protective love for the creation that would be unimaginably more meaningful and joyful than our present destructive and wasteful economy. The absence of the vast apparatus of human society, that made me so uneasy last night, now begins to be a comfort to me. I am afoot in the woods. I am alive in the world, this moment, without the help or the interference of any machine. I can move without reference to anything except the lay of the land and the capabilities of my own body. The necessities of foot travel in this steep country have stripped away all superfluities. I simply could not enter into this place and assume its quiet with all the belongings of a family man, property holder, etc. For the time, I am reduced to my irreducible self. I feel the lightness of body that a man must feel who has just lost fifty pounds of fat. As I leave the bare expanse of the rock and go in under the trees again, I am aware that I move in the landscape as one of its little details, inundated by the life of the woods.

Walking through the woods, you can never see far, either

ahead or behind, so you move without much of a sense of getting anywhere or of moving at any certain speed. You burrow through the foliage in the air much as a mole burrows through the roots in the ground. The views that open out occasionally from the ridges afford a relief, a recovery of orientation, that they could never give as mere "scenery," looked at from a turnout at the edge of a highway.

The trail leaves the ridge and goes down a ravine into the valley of a creek where the night chill has stayed. I pause only long enough to drink the cold clean water. The trail climbs up onto the next ridge.

It is the ebb of the year. Though the slopes have not yet taken on the bright colors of the autumn maples and oaks, some of the duller trees are already shedding. The foliage has begun to flow down the cliff faces and the slopes like a tide pulling back. The woods is mostly quiet, subdued, as if the pressure of survival has grown heavy upon it, as if above the growing warmth of the day the cold of winter can be felt waiting to descend.

At my approach a big hawk flies off the low branch of an oak and out over the treetops. An amazing precision in getting such a spread of wings out through the close webbing of the branches so swiftly. Now and again a nuthatch hoots, off somewhere in the woods. Twice I stop and watch an ovenbird. A few feet ahead of me there is a sudden movement in the leaves, and then quiet. When I slip up and examine the spot there is nothing to be found. Whatever passed there has disappeared, quicker than the hand that is quicker than the eye, a shadow

fallen into a shadow.

In the afternoon I leave the trail. My walk so far has come perhaps three-quarters of the way around a long zigzagging loop that will eventually bring me back to my starting place. Now I turn down a small unnamed branch of the creek where I am camped. And now I begin the loveliest part of the day. There is nothing here resembling a trail. The best way is nearly always to follow the edge of the stream, stepping from one stone to another. Crossing back and forth over the water, stepping on or over rocks and logs, the way ahead is never clear for more than a few feet. The stream accompanies me down, threading its way under boulders and logs and over little falls and rapids. The rhododendron overhangs it so closely in places that I can only go by stooping. Over the rhododendron are the great dark heads of the hemlocks. The streambanks are ferny and mossy. And through this green tunnel the voice of the stream works its bemused changes from rock to rock; subdued like all the other autumn voices of the woods, it seems sunk in a deep contented meditation on the sounds of *l*.

The water in the pools is absolutely clear. If it weren't for the shadows and ripples you would hardly notice that it is water; the fish would seem to swim in the air. As it is, where there is no leaf floating, it is impossible to tell exactly where the plane of the surface lies. As I walk up on a pool the little fish dart every which way out of sight. And then after I sit still a while, watching, they come out again. Their shadows flow over the rocks and leaves on the bottom. Now I have come into the heart of the woods. I am far from the highway and can hear no sound of it. All around there is a grand deep autumn quiet, in which a few insects dream their summer songs.

Suddenly a wren sings way off in the underbrush. A red-breasted nuthatch walks, hooting, headfirst down the trunk of a walnut. An ovenbird walks out along the limb of a hemlock and looks at me, curious. The little fish soar in the pool, turning their clean quick angles, their shadows seeming barely to keep up. As I lean and dip my cup in the water, they scatter. I drink, and go on.

When I get back to camp it is only the middle of the afternoon or a little after. Since I left in the morning I have walked something like eight miles. I haven't hurried—have mostly poked along, stopping often and looking around. But I am tired, and coming down the creek I have got both feet wet. I find a sunny place, and take off my shoes and socks and set them to dry. For a long time then, lying propped against the trunk of a tree, I read and rest and watch the evening come.

All day I have moved through the woods, making as little noise as possible. Slowly my mind and my nerves have wound down to a walking pace. The quiet of the woods has ceased to be something that I observe; now it is something that I am a part of. I have joined it with my own quiet. As the twilight draws on I no longer feel the strangeness and uneasiness of the evening before. The sounds of the creek move through my mind as they move through the valley, unimpeded and clear.

When the time comes I prepare supper and eat, and then wash kettle and cup and spoon and put them away. As far as possible I get things ready for an early start in the morning. Soon after dark I go to bed, and I sleep well.

I waken long before dawn. The air is warm and I feel

rested and wide awake. By the light of a small candle lantern I break camp and pack. And then I begin the steep climb back to the car.

The moon is bright and high. The woods stands in deep shadow, the light falling soft through the openings of the foliage. The trees appear immensely tall, and black, gravely looming over the path. It is windless and still; the moonlight pouring over the country seems more potent than the air. All around me there is still that constant low singing of the insects. For days now it has continued without letup or inflection, like ripples on water under a steady breeze. While I slept it went on through the night, a shimmer on my mind. My shoulder brushes a low tree overhanging the path and a bird that was asleep on one of the branches startles awake and flies off into the shadows, and I go on with the sense that I am passing near to the sleep of things.

In a way this is the best part of the trip. Stopping now and again to rest, I linger over it, sorry to be going. It seems to me that if I were to stay on, today would be better than yesterday, and I realize it was to renew the life of that possibility that I came here. What I am leaving is something to look forward to.

CHAPTER FOUR *The Unforeseen Wilderness*

That the world is stable and its order fixed is perhaps the most persistent human delusion. How many errors have been made on the assumption that what was *is?* To a young child the house he lives in is permanant and unchanging, an eternal verity. But it is clear to the man who keeps the house that if it is treated as an eternal verity it will soon perish altogether. Against the constant jeopardy of decay there is the necessity of constant renewal. And there are, of course, the maxims to the effect that you cannot go home again, or step into the same river twice.

I knew all that as well, I suppose, as any other man of my age. But as soon as I was confronted with the new experience of the Red River Gorge I immediately fell into the old error, assuming that the place partook of the nature of its maps— that, for instance, from what I knew I could predict what I would learn, or that my experience could be made to go according to a plan. Like a good engineer, I wanted to foresee what I was going to do and then do it.

But perhaps the first lesson we have to learn, or relearn, from a wilderness is that the creation does not live and change according to a plan, but by freely accommodating what happens to it. The wild creatures do not go to some appointed place such as a kitchen or a restaurant to eat, but eat what they find where they find it. The bends and bars and pools of the river are not foreordained, but are made in response to obstructions and openings.

To a river, as to any natural force, an obstruction is merely an opportunity. For the river's nature is to flow; it is not just spatial in dimension, but temporal as well. All things must yield to the impulse of the water *in time*, if not today then tomorrow or in a thousand years. If its way is obstructed then it goes around the obstruction or under it or over it and, flowing past it, wears it away. Men may dam it and say that they have made a lake, but it will still be a river. It will keep its nature and bide its time, like a caged wild animal alert for the slightest opening. In time it will have its way; the dam like the ancient cliffs will be carried away piecemeal in the currents.

The engineer's assumption that the nature of a place is fixed and can be altered according to plan is an illusion, as has been too often proven when planned "improvements" have produced wholly unforeseen disasters. But the engineer's illusion, in our time, is an illusion backed by enormous powers of technology and politics and wealth, and an illusion so empowered preserves itself by becoming an institution. It has a much longer life than the illusions of persons, and before it dies it may do, and usually does, long-term damage. The engineering illusion has produced damage, as in the strip mines of Eastern Kentucky, that will require a geologic era to correct.

To a modern engineer, entering a landscape with bull-
dozers, power shovels, dynamite, and the other tools of his

trade, the blueprint must seem as absolute as the will of God. A kindred, if smaller, illusion brought the pioneer plowman onto the steep slopes: the manifest destiny of a plowman was to plow; the tool, the human possibility, was the point of reference, not the nature of the place. When the dam has silted up and a valley is destroyed for the foreseeable future, or when the plowed-up topsoil has washed away and the watershed is ruined, it is too late. The plans have been undone by natural processes that were not foreseen or taken into account. But it is the business of natural processes to produce consequences, and the first law of ecology is that justice is *always* done—though not necessarily to those who deserve it. Ecological justice, in fact, falls most often on later generations, or on the people who live downwind or downstream.

But the man who goes into the wilderness on foot, stripped of all the devices of the illusion of fixed order, finds his assumptions to be much shorter lived. Afoot, cut off from the powers by which men change things, he has made himself vulnerable to change. Whether he intends it or not, the wilderness receives him as a student. And what it begins to teach him is how to live beyond his expectations; if he returns often and stays long perhaps it will teach him to live *without* expectations. It will teach him the wisdom of taking no thought for the morrow—not because taking thought is a bad idea, but because it is not possible; he doesn't know what thought tomorrow will require.

The lessons are everywhere. He can't avoid them. They are innate in the experience. The weather and the mood of the woods have changed since his last trip. The stepping-stones on which he crossed the creek a month ago are now washed away. The pebbles and small stones of the stream bed have moved and changed, and in their changing he feels the changing of the boulders and the cliffs. If the weather on his last trip was so pleasant as to have stayed in his mind, an enticement to come back, he may be discouraged this trip to have to contend with sweltering heat, or with a cold rain. But the elusive ovenbird, that he sort of expected never to see, suddenly appears on a low limb beside the path. Or a pair of grouse erupt in flight almost under his feet, causing his heart to jump out of place—and for the next hundred yards he walks unconsciously on tiptoe, scarcely breathing, alert to what is around him as he has rarely been. Or a turn in the path shows him suddenly a rare flame azalea in bloom. What he planned is not happening, as if by some natural law. He is finding the *life* of the time, the challenges and delights, in what he did not foresee.

No place is to be learned like a textbook or a course in school, and then turned away from forever on the assumption that one's knowledge of it is complete. What is to be known about it is without limit, and it is endlessly changing. Knowing it is therefore like breathing: it can happen, it stays real, only on the condition that it *continue* to happen. As soon as it is recognized that a river—or, for that matter, a home—is not a place but a process, not a fact but an event, there ought to come an immense relief: one can step into the same river twice, one can go home again.

We had spent a hot, hard July afternoon tramping in the Gorge in search of a place we had heard about, and we had failed to find it. The foliage closed in around us like a heavy fog, and we were drenched with sweat and with rainwater from an earlier shower that clung all that humid afternoon to the leaves. From the standpoint of our expectations the afternoon was a total loss, better forgotten. Except that in the midst of that failed search we *happened* on something unforgettable: a little dell in the woods where several streams met, making a pattern like a chicken track. The air opened and grew spacious under great hemlocks and beeches; shafts of sunlight slanted in as thick as the tree trunks; we rested there, and found cool water to drink. It is printed on my memory, a sort of blessing, by the force of its unexpectedness. Though our search failed in its intention, it succeeded in one of its accidents.

One Memorial Day—or as it turned out, one Memorable Day—I started out to canoe the Upper Gorge by myself, putting in below the bridge where Highway 746 crosses the Red. I had previously been down only a little below the mouth of Stillwater Creek, and so I had no idea what I was undertaking.

The river was high, the water about the depth of a paddle blade over the riffles. For a while I went down fast and easy. The current was strong even in the pools, and I was getting what I thought to be a free ride.

I had the river all to myself. As I went down wood ducks rose off the water ahead of me and flew downstream. I saw several water thrushes. I found a phoebe's nest with four fledged young on an overhanging rock face about a foot above the water.

And then I came to the first big rapid about a mile below Stillwater. There the river broke, falling steeply, through a narrow opening between two huge rocks, and above the rocks *57* the slopes rose almost vertically, thickly covered with trees and undergrowth. I tied up first on one side of the river and then the other, and took a long look around.

The uproar of the rapid filled and beat inside my head, seeming to accumulate; I was rapidly becoming unable, as the saying is, to hear myself think. It was as though I had been brought suddenly, ignorant of the proper etiquette, into the presence of a grand and austere personage who had taken my life into his hands. I was losing my confidence and poise. The river was defeating me, and what is more it was making me glad to accept defeat. This rapid was bad, and I knew that it promised worse. I no longer had the faintest shadow of a wish to go any farther. And yet my pride held on to my intentions a while longer, and I carefully considered every possibility of getting through.

After much looking and pondering and looking back I was happy to conclude that there were no arguments at all in favor of going on. Running the rapid seemed a stupid risk for one man, and a portage looked about equally impossible. There was nothing to do but turn around and go out the way I had come in. It took me nearly four hours to make it back to my starting place, wading and pulling the canoe against the swift current. At times the water became too deep to wade, and I would have to swim across, or drift back downstream to where I could wade across. It was something of an ordeal, and I knew at the time that I was in considerable danger: in water like that, plunging under and around big rocks and sunken trees, there are any number of ways to drown.

But the real austerity of the Upper Gorge, and the extremity of my misjudgment in attempting it alone, didn't dawn on me until some weeks later. Mr. Wendell Nickell of West Liberty had taken me down the cliff to the Dog Drowning Hole, perhaps two miles below the rapid where I had turned back on my canoe trip. There had been rain and again the river was swollen; we could hear its clamor while we were still high up on the face of the cliff. When we finally worked our way down to the edge of it we were submerged in its sound. Its great noise, the voice of the whole stream, was so disproportionate to anything we could *see* that, within it, the river seemed to churn past us in silence. It drove down onto the comb of the rocks and was torn apart, buried in white froth, and then it gathered back into the single strand of itself, to be torn apart again.

Dog Drowning Hole indeed! The thought of drowning was native there. One could hardly look at it without knowing how it could tread down the head of a swimmer and hold it, while the great voice drumming there between the cliffs would go on, exuberant and oblivious, unchanged. It was a tenuous margin we stood on, the wall of the Gorge at our backs, and at our feet the let-loose tromping and churning of the Dog Drowning Hole.

And then while we stood there watching, my guide said very casually: "If three men were down in here, and one broke his leg, the other two couldn't carry him out."

I suppose that until somebody has tried it we won't know for sure about that—but I saw his point. As though his words had nudged me finally beyond the frontier of my ignorance, the reality of the Gorge suddenly stood up in all my nerves, and

I realized what an edge I had come to on my canoe trip. When I pushed off that morning I passed ahead of my intentions as a driver speeding at night will overdrive his lights. If I had somehow contrived to go on past the rapid where I had turned back, I would have passed beyond what I could imagine, there would have been no foreseeing what might have happened. Before, the Gorge had been a place I understood somewhat as I understood its maps. But now it became a presence that I felt in the roots of my hair and the pit of my stomach, as though something whose existence I had failed to anticipate had come up behind me in the dark and touched the back of my neck.

One way to see the Red River is by canoe. That way one sees it from the perspective of water, having made common cause with it, to be carried by it. Drifting, there comes an intimate sense of how the water has sought its way through the country, and one feels how simple and steadfast is its obedience to the law of gravity, filling and flowing on.

Another way is by foot. Step into the river at the bridge on Highway 746 and wade down through the Gorge to the bridge on Highway 715. You wade because the slopes on either shore are so steep and so thickly overgrown that the best walkway is obviously the bed of the river. And the perspective of the walker is as radically different from that of the boatman as it is from that of the stander on the bank. Walking, you have not merely entered the water; you have entered the course of the stream. You are experiencing not the stream alone nor the land alone, but the contending of the two by which each has been shaped. You are encountering by touch as well as by sight the water of the river and the obstacles it makes its way through or over or under or around. You have put your body into it like a gauge to measure the variations of its depth and the changes of its flow.

There are certain personal considerations to be dealt with at first. You are necessarily wet to the waist from the start, and you know you are *going* to be wet to the waist for hours on end. And there is the strangeness of walking over a surface that you can feel but cannot see; in spite of the use of a walking stick, the most reliable device for detecting submerged boulders and logs turns out to be your shinbone. As soon as these are accepted as normal circumstances you can give your attention to the adventure. And it is an adventure. One of the best.

Canoeing down a flowing stream, no matter in what mood it is done, never quite escapes the impulse of the current. Loitering or stopping, you nevertheless remain answerable to the movement of the water, the necessity to be going on. But walking down the Red, through the roughs of its Upper Gorge, has nothing in common with flowing; the current when it becomes swift enough to be noticeable is not an asset but a difficulty. Walking is slow and considering and deliberate. There is no building in its momentum. Where the canoeist could stop only with some forethought and considerable effort, where he would find it simpler and easier to go on, the walker always finds it easier to stop.

And so walking down through the Upper Gorge, we no   *61*

sooner become involved in our trip, than we become equally involved in its side trips and diversions. We find phoebes' nests on the rocks—two that are empty, one with two eggs. When we stop and listen we hear warblers singing everywhere. We linger over the rock gardens along the shores, examining their growth of lichens and mosses and liverworts, violets and bluets and rue. The laurel bushes that here and there overhang the banks are in bloom. Once we see a frog clinging to a rock face like a little patch of lichen. On the bed of the river in the shallows we see fish's nests of heaped up pebbles.

We shed our packs at the mouth of one of the smaller tributary streams and, feeling light and quick-footed without our loads, pass back into the valley wall. The branch enters the river through a deep narrow cut beneath overhanging ledges and the close foliage of rhododendron—a kind of burrow that leads us back and up over preliminary steps in the rock ledges. And then the foliage opens overhead and withdraws on either side. It is a little as though we have emerged on the bottom of a well, but the space is broad and lofty, the proportions those of a great temple. In front of us there is a series of narrow ledges, divided by sheer high falls of the rock. From the top ledge, high up against the sky, a little stream leaps and slides, glittering and spattering, until finally it is gathered again into the tidy stream at our feet. The ledges are all covered and hung with flowers and mosses and ferns. On the other sides of the opening the forest rises tall and densely green. It is the wildest of places, the long casual violence of its making still potent in it. And yet it is pleasing in the way that the greatest architecture is pleasing, as though its shape and proportions were the result of superb calculation. We stand in its shade and its looming gentle quiet, and look. And then we reenter the stream's dark burrow.

And trash. We see plenty of trash—old tires, buckets and bottles and cans, the various plastic conveniences of our disposable civilization, leftovers of what Edward Abbey calls the world's "grossest national product." We see trash that has floated down out of upriver dumps, and trash that has been carried in by campers who would no doubt have got equal enjoyment if they had pitched their tents in the parking lot of a drive-in restaurant. Farther down, where the river begins to be accompanied by foot trails, we will see piles of excrement that might be the sign of some large wild animal were they not surrounded by lavish blossoms of pink toilet paper.

To be ashamed of one's species is a strange and sickening emotion. It goes against the deepest instincts of kinship and self-regard. And yet it is an emotion that I—and I think a great many others—have to contend with more and more often. When I think of the near-perfection of industrial and recreational pollution, of the near-universality of armed hatred and prejudice, of our scientists' ecstatic dance in the light of the first atomic explosion, of the utter destruction of land for its timber or coal—then I feel such a heavy disgust that I look at the so-called lower animals with envy. I would gladly give up several of the larger benefits of "progress" for the assurance that none of my kind had ever subjugated another people or destroyed a mountain or a watershed or napalmed a child. When I look at these lower animals and consider that not one of them ever destroyed its own habitat, or poisoned its own food and water, I am astonished at the claims we make for the "higher" human intelligence. The lowest animal, at present, is man.

I would try to get rid of such emotions if I did not recognize their truth. In these times they are a part of the responsibility of an honest person. I believe that I would be a dangerous man if I did *not* feel them.

The evil that has produced what we now call the "environmental crisis" is arrogance or, to use the ancient Greek term that is more accurate, *hubris*, the assumption by men of divine prerogatives. It is the willingness to use more power than one can control. It is the ignorant use of power. It is a sin the consequences of which are invariably visited upon the descendants of the sinner, as the Greek myths and tragedies tell us over and over again. It is the reason why humility and modesty and self-restraint and temperance have been recognized as essential virtues through all of human history. The man who assumes and uses the powers of the gods must in his ignorance inevitably reduce the common fund of life and fortune on which his children will have to live.

The cure for *hubris* is an exact understanding of what are the powers and prerogatives of a *man*. Men who become too powerful and too proud, too arrogant in their use of the world, are beaten down, reduced to mansize, driven back into their proper estate. That is a divine—or, if you would prefer, a natural—law. It is one of the major subjects of *The Odyssey:*
64 Odysseus, for his offense against Poseidon, is stripped of

everything—homeland and rank and followers and weapons and clothes—and made to contend naked against the sea, not as a king but as a man, inferior to the gods and therefore dependent upon them. In the same way, as John Stewart Collis shows in his excellent book *The Triumph of the Tree*, nations of people who destroy the forests that protect the steep slopes and safeguard the health of watersheds, destroy at the same time the sources of their life, and eventually famine drives them out at large into the world. Perhaps the cutters of the trees do not themselves suffer for what they have done. Perhaps they prosper and their work seems productive only of wealth. But they have nevertheless prepared a justice which descends to their children like a congenital disease.

We have entered the environmental crisis with an arrogance and a power that are without precedent, just as the envisionable catastrophes are without precedent. We are no longer faced with the loss of a kingdom or the conversion of fertile cropland into desert. Now we face cosmic disaster: the extinction of human life, and of all other life associated with it. For it may be that our species has now implemented its power and pride on such a scale, swelled so far out of its proper place in the ecological order that it can be forced back into its true limits—the limits of creatures and mortals—only by its destruction.

There is another kind of trial.

There are the trials imposed by the gods or by natural forces on men who have unwittingly deserved them, usually by forgetting that they live in a wilderness universe in which consequences are unforeseeable, and in which humility is therefore the first virtue. But there are also trials that are assumed wittingly, and perhaps by these assumed trials one may hope to avoid the harsher trials that are imposed.

A man may cast himself off from the comforts and securities of civilization as he knows it and enter the wilderness, taking with him only what he can carry on his back. He may begin with plans, but as soon as he leaves the roads and the beaten paths he is perforce contending at every step with the unforeseen. He may have come for fun, and he may in fact take from the experience an intense pleasure, but he is nevertheless being tried. He is forced to live within his own personal limits, for he has left behind the machines and the devices that amplify his power. In the wilderness he can go only so far as his own legs will carry him, he can take with him only as large a load as his own back will bear. He finds that he has a smaller place and a smaller part to play in creation than he thought, but he finds—and this is his reward—that they are large enough. He should discover, at the very least, that a man who has a body and five senses to amuse himself with has little need for the machinery of recreation. The time he stays in the wilderness is a time spent in touch with a nonhuman world that is mysterious to him. From the flowers to the stars he sees little or nothing that men have made. He spends that time not as a master of the world but as a dweller in it—which is, after all, his true condition. And he should emerge from his experience somewhat changed—less eager to cash in on his birthright, aware that men are *part* of what they destroy.

Certain Indian youths, when they were ready to enter into the estate of manhood, would undergo willingly and wittingly a man-imposed trial, and they did this for the express purpose of avoiding those trials that are imposed by the gods or by nature. My authority here is Clark Wissler's *Indians of the United States*. When the Indian youth "seeks wisdom and light," Wissler says, "he goes out alone and, deep in the presence of nature, opens his mind and heart. He may fast and even tear his flesh, crying out, 'Oh, pity me! Oh, pity me!'—believing that the unseen powers are human and that they may be moved to grant him security and power . . . after fasting and torturing himself for a long time, a man . . . may hear a voice, and in the darkness a shape may appear. It may be an animal, a bird or even a tree, but eventually it becomes a human being, addressing the supplicant with an inquiry as to why he is crying there. If his request is granted, instructions are given the supplicant, songs are taught him and certain injunctions laid upon him. The grant of power may be immunity from disease or from injury in war, or power to heal the sick. Such powers are usually specific and not general.

. . . . A bond or pledge is made by which the individual in question is linked to a particular unseen power . . . upon whom he may call in case of need. The song and the formula are passwords, so to speak, which reach the ear of the unseen. If the vision were that of a bear which spoke as a man, then that animal becomes the symbol of power, and the fortunate recipient may carry about with him an image of a bear, a claw, bone or piece of skin."

Whereas our society is discordant both within itself and within the natural environment, the Indian societies were for the most part harmonious within themselves and within nature. And it seems to me that one of the keys to that harmony, and undoubtedly one of its sources, was this initiatory trial by which, in order to become a man, a youth went alone into the wilderness to discover by going without it for a time the meaning of his society, to discover in humility his own smallness in the world of nature and his dependence on it, and to bring back finally some mark, which he would bear through life, of his unity with that larger world, some password by which to reach "the ear of the unseen." One became a man, that is, not by becoming presumptuous and proud in the use of human powers as is the tendency with us, but by the recognition and acceptance of one's human limits, by acknowledging one's dependence on powers beyond human reach.

I think that defines even for us—or especially for us—the usefulness and the necessity of the wilderness. Cut off from the wilderness, confined strictly to our cities and highways and croplands where we may persuade ourselves to feel safe in the illusion of human dominion, where will we go to learn to be as humble as we need to be? Without the wilderness to teach us, without the willingness to go and learn what it alone has the power to teach, we can only become more dangerous to the world and to ourselves.

What would it be like to experience the Red River unspoiled by men's abuse and refuse? Perhaps those of us living now will never know. Perhaps we may learn from our errors, in time, and become civilized enough to preserve and care for such places. Perhaps that is an exceedingly small possibility. At any rate, now the traveler in the Gorge will find that to get his experience of it pure he must be continuously editing out the most damning evidence against his species. It is a modern hardship.

And there is an ancient hardship. As motorists we are accustomed to journeys that occur in different places but not in different conditions. A man might drive his car across the Salt Lake Desert and then across Salt Lake City, and the condition of both trips would be that of the automobile; what his predecessors in covered wagons knew of the desert is simply lost to him. Going afoot through the Upper Gorge, we have reverted to an ancient mode and mentality of travel. We are experiencing the place as a condition. And as the day goes on that condition gets livelier and more assertive. We become weary, the packs heavy, the footwork more and more burdened by the water and the hidden obstacles of the river. We begin looking for a campsite.

Perhaps there are places in the world where Nature has provided comfortable campsites a day's walk apart. In the Red River Gorge Nature had her mind on other work. It is a long time, and a long way, after we have decided to stop before we finally come to a stopping place. But there is a compensation, a sort of justice, operative in this—not the elusive justice of desert and reward, but the unfailing natural symmetry of cause and effect. The longer and harder the labor has been, the gladder you are to rest, the more intricately satisfying are all the details of the day's end: taking off the pack, changing to dry clothes and shoes and socks, resting, eating, looking around. Sitting and looking around is somehow the best of it. All day we have been in motion ourselves, and now we sit very still and watch the motions of the world: the flight of birds, the stirrings of the wind, the flowing of the river, the darkening of the day. In our weariness and stillness we watch it happen without impatience, with candid interest. It is as gratifying as watching somebody else work.

We have put in a hard day, and we have come to a good place: a smooth sand beach opposite the mouth of Solomon Branch. Towering over us, in the downstream angle between the branch and the river, is a big rust-red point of rock. While we make camp the last of the sunlight glows on this rock and then slowly rises away from it. There seems little likelihood of rain and we decide against the use of shelters, which would be hard to secure there on the open beach anyhow, and simply unroll our beds on the sand. We cook and eat and loaf and talk and finally, with the night cooling on our faces, sleep.

We are awakened a little after daylight by the calling and answering of the phoebes who live on the red cliff above us. We have breakfast, and then loaf around, waiting for the dew to dry off our bedding. Or that is one reason we put off starting. Another is that we have the hardest going still ahead of us, and we know it.

This is the day of the Roughs of the Red. The course of the river becomes choked with tremendous stones—no longer the boulder here and there of other parts of the river, but piles and barricades of boulders. Our day's journey resolves into a series of problems and solutions. We thread our way around a pool too deep to wade, climbing and stooping and straddling

and crawling over and around and through a sprawl of big

rocks that makes us feel like ants in a gravel pile. We cross
swift deep water on stepping-stones the size of automobiles
that lie *almost* more than a man's stride apart. We work our
way around one side of a large pool, only to discover that we
can't pass that way, and we have to work our way back and
try the other side. The way is never clear very far ahead. We
keep seeing, just ahead of us, barriers that it seems to us only
water could get through. Always in sight around us are the
marks of the power of flowing water: the tumbled and sculp-
tured stones, driftlogs lodged in the branches of trees and on
the tops of boulders many feet above our heads. We can never
quite forget here that we are traveling through the workplace
of a great creative force, one of the methods of which is rampage.

A man's way through a wilderness he is familiar with has
something of the nature of art; it keeps an abiding reference
to knowledge and to previous use. Today we are far removed
from men's ways, and are learning something of the way of
nature. There are no paths going our way, and as a trail the
river has become capricious and deceptive. We go through
its stone maze much as the water goes through it, moving
easily through the open places, pausing at the barriers to hunt
a way through, and then passing, released, relieved, through
the opening we have found, going on. Discovering the way for
ourselves, we begin to feel that we are not simply *in* the
wilderness, but that we are *part* of it, moving within it in direct
response to it, moving as it requires us to move and as it
moves. Our journey has become one of its processes.

This is a stretch of country that might have been deliber-
ately meant to refute all our idle talk about "the everlasting
hills." There are no everlasting hills. There is only ever-

lasting process. Here the hills are clearly being torn down. But this, I keep reminding myself, is not destruction. It is creation. If men, with their souped-up ambitions and their panic-stricken sense of time, should attempt to work on such a scale—and they do—the invariable result would be destruction. But this is a scene, and a result, of the creation—which simply cannot be thought of in man's terms. It is never—except in his limited and selfish view—destructive. It is never going through a period of destruction between something created in the past and something to be created in the future. It is always creating what *is*.

It is our journey, our laborious passage through these works, that has taught us this. Passing down, contriving against obstacles, as the water passes, we have moved outside ourselves into a curious sympathy with what is happening here. We have dealt with it stone by stone. And so we do not now stand apart from it like real estate speculators, saying what a nice place it will be when it is finished. For we know that it *is* finished, just as it was, and as it will be. We know that only a fragment of its substance and its duration is visible to us, and that however tumultuous and chaotic the place may look it is involved in a process that is ever coherent and whole. For the wilderness, which is to say the universe, we have no words. We deal with its stones, its trees, its water. We ask ourselves which will be the best way to go. Our words are for the way we have been.

In the very depths of the Roughs, we find standing in the stream a craggy stone with bluets and liverworts in bloom on it, and a few ferns. It is not large—perhaps six or eight feet in diameter, and standing three or four feet above the surface.

What stops us and keeps us standing there, looking and looking, is that it is a complete landscape, a rocky mountain landscape, exquisitely scaled and proportioned and colored, as though contrived and placed there by the most subtle of Japanese gardeners. It is uncannily all of a piece, orderly, impeccable. Like a fine work of art or a neat small farm, it is resonant with the intimation of orders too large and too small to see.

We camp that night at the head of a foot trail that will take us down to the concrete bridge on Highway 715, where we have left a car. To get there in the morning, after our days in the river, will seem a short easy walk. The rough going is all behind us now. As trials go, ours has been mostly a pleasure trip. And yet it has been difficult enough, far enough from roads and paths, to carry us beyond our usual lives into intimate touch, a sort of association, with the wild river. Though we have been gone only two days, and have never been more than a few miles from the paved road, our journey has about it the aura of great distance and long time. I lie down to sleep feeling accomplished and satisfied. I look back on our journey with a great liking. And having been so far outside myself, I find to my relief that I am glad to be back, eager to be going home.

In the morning I wake before daylight, and lie still, looking and listening. The night fades. For a while I hear in the distance the voice of one whippoorwill. And then the day birds.

CHAPTER FIVE *The Journey's End*

Five years have passed since I first looked out over the Red River country from the fire tower on Pine Ridge. During that time I have come to know a little. I think of the growth of that knowledge, small as it is, as one of the landmarks of my life—a happening both large and altogether good. I have spent not a single moment there that I look back on with regret. I have not a single feeling about it that is vague or uncertain. My times there answer to memory with a purity and clarity that is like the water of its streams. For all my remaining ignorance of it, for all in it that is dark, I think of it as a *clear* place.

At first I experienced mostly its strangeness. I remember the curious uneasiness I would feel, then, when I went any distance off the trails. It was not that I was lost. But the lay of the land was strange to me and when I cast myself loose in it, certain as I might be of where I was, I would begin to feel lost. Sometimes my return to the trail would partake somewhat of the nature of a retreat, the Unknown having surrounded me on three sides and begun to close in.

I thought of it then as a strange place, a place strange *to me*. The presumptuousness of that, it now occurs to me, is probably a key to the destructiveness that has characterized the whole history of the white man's relation to the American wilderness. For it is presumptuous, entirely so, to enter a place for the first time and pronounce it strange. Strange to whom? Certainly to its own creatures—to the birds and animals and insects and fish and snakes, to the human family I know that lives knowingly and lovingly there—it is not strange. To them as it was to the Indians who once lived in its caves and in the bottomlands near its creek mouths it is daily reality, regular stuff.

To call a place strange in the presence of its natives is bad manners at best. At worst, it partakes of the fateful arrogance of those explorers who familiarize the "strange" places they come to by planting in them the alien flag of the place they have left, and who have been followed, always, by the machinery of conquest and exploitation and destruction.

The strangeness, as I recognized after a while, for I went in flying no flag and riding no machine, was all in me. It was my own strangeness that I felt, for I was a man out of place. And I believe that only in that realization lay the possibility that I would come to know the Red River Gorge even a little. If I had continued to look upon the place as strange I would clearly have had only two choices: stay out of it altogether, or change it, destroy it as I found it and make it into something else. But once I learned to look upon myself as a stranger there it became possible for me to return again and again without preaching to the natives, or making treaties with them, or swindling them out of their property, or cutting down any timber, or buying a lot on which to build a drive-in restaurant. It became possible for me to leave the place as it is, to want it to be as it is, to be quiet in it, to learn about it and from it. Lacking any such disciplining and humbling sense of being strangers, wanderers away from home, the European conquerors entered America like so many English sparrows or Japanese beetles, free of controls, cultural or natural, that would have brought their lives into harmony with this land. And they and their descendants have lived here for the most part as strangers, and for the most part out of control, ever since. And now, by "generously" gospelizing the technology of exploitation and waste, they are teaching other peoples how to be strangers, even in their own homes.

Slowly, almost imperceptibly, the experience of strangeness was transformed into the experience of familiarity. The place did not become predictable; the more I learned of it, the less predictable it seemed. But my visits began to define themselves in terms of recurrences and recognitions that were pleasant in themselves, and that set me free in the place. I began to depart from the trails with a comfortable notion of where the contour of a slope or the fall of a stream would be likely to take me. Better than that, I soon began to think that there could not be many better places to get lost in. And finally—to my regret, as it turned out—I realized that, as much crossed as that country is by roads and trails, it is very likely impossible to get lost in it, at least not for long at a time.

Its mysteries remained—for though we pretend otherwise, the unknown increases with the known. But mystery is not the same as strangeness. A mystery can be familiar. In this scientific age, when our "practical intelligence" gropes so destructively toward the "use" of everything, we should remember that it is possible to be comfortably ignorant. It is possible, and I am sure it will prove to be necessary, to make peace with what we cannot understand.

As my knowledge of the place grew I began to have a sense of the meaning—or the anti-meaning—of its planned destruction, which carried me far beyond the mere principles of conservation and preservation. I began to feel in the presence and substance of its life the complexity and the magnitude of its death. And I realized that in the story of the Gorge I had forsaken the role, and the immunity, of an observer. Or rather that role had forsaken me, for I had become personally involved. The death of the Gorge, for some of my fellow Kentuckians, would be merely an act of "progress"—a cause that they may themselves be dying for. But to me, because I *knew* something of what would die, it would be a great personal loss. It was too late to be objective. I had spent some of my best days there, not as an observer or writer but as a creature bemused by the creation. The Gorge had become part of my life. I knew that whether I continued to go there or not it would remain meaningful and important to me. I knew that there would be a certain irreplaceable comfort that I would draw from the knowledge that it was preserved and cherished and enjoyed by members of my species.

And the more I saw and understood of the condition of the watershed and of the river itself, the more clear it seemed to me that the damming of the Gorge would be not only destructive and meaningless, but useless upon the very terms of the argument for its destruction: the conditions that are responsible for flooding will cause the rapid siltation and destruction of the proposed reservoir; the conditions that bring water shortages into prospect for the downstream cities preclude the possibility that these shortages will be forestalled for very long by the building of reservoirs.

It is a fact that the entire Kentucky River system, which the central part of the state complacently depends upon for its future water supply, is deteriorating rapidly because of strip mining, because of bad farming, because of industrial and agricultural pollutants, because of urban sewage, because of insane agricultural policies that force small farmers to overuse their land in order to secure a bare survival while rich "agri-businessmen" are highly paid not to use their land at all. It is deteriorating, that is to say, because almost nobody cares, or cares to know, where water comes from, so long as it keeps coming. The going assumption is that people so ignorant and thoughtless and silly and greedy may simply call upon the Army Corps of Engineers in order to receive a clean and abundant supply of water from reservoirs in the mountains. A much likelier outcome is that they will be drinking an ever stronger mixture of sewage and mine acid and mud and cropspray and various other defecations of the industrial paradise.

The proposed dam in the Red River Gorge is not the definitive solution to any problem, upstream or down. Like many another project that has been offered to the people as a lasting monument of human progress, it is an illusion, expedient and temporary, that will only delay, perhaps catastrophically, the achievement of a real solution. It is a cheap shortcut. And in the art of earth-keeping, as in any other art, shortcuts always leave out essential steps. If the destruction of the steep land of the watershed were stopped; if that land were adequately forested and grassed, as it could be in a comparatively short time; if sane methods were made to prevail in mining and forestry and agriculture—that work alone would go far toward assuring an adequate water supply from the Kentucky River. And flood control on the scale now contemplated would certainly become unnecessary. Seriously damaging floods of the Kentucky River are a modern phenomenon. They are manmade, caused by the abuse of the watershed. As evidence, I need cite only the fact that well into this century, in the lower part of the valley, houses were confidently built upon sites that now are flooded about every ten years. Flood control as we now know it is no more than a subsidization of the crimes and abuses of the exploiters, the burden as usual falling upon innocent tax payers.

Upon their utterly disreputable argument of "use" the Engineers and the pushers of "development" have erected the even more disreputable argument of "recreation." For in addition to putting nature to man's work, a dam, they say, will put it to his pleasure. Modern Americans, as we all know, are crowded and stifled in the cities, and are therefore most excruciatingly in need of recreation. And what is to be the form of this recreation? Why, it is to be crowded and stifled in the country. Relief from the suburbs of brick and bedford stone is to be found in suburbs of canvas and aluminum. Relief from traffic in the streets is to be sought amid traffic on a lake. The harried city dweller, who has for fifty weeks coveted his neighbor's house and his neighbor's wife, may now soothe his nerves for two weeks in coveting his neighbor's trailer and his neighbor's boat—also in putting up with his neighbor's children, listening to his neighbor's radio, breathing his neighbor's smoke, walking on his neighbor's broken bottles. While he is doing all these things he is surrounded by "the beauty of nature," which is a big item in recreation. And a lake, the developers agree, provides a lot more beauty of nature than a river because it has room for more and bigger and faster boats, making it possible for more people to see more beauty of nature in less time. It really takes a lot of beauty of nature to make up for the smoke and smog of our stifling cities, and so if it only takes ten minutes to go in a boat where it once took all day to go on foot that's all to the good. Why be satisfied with mere yards of natural beauty when you can have *miles* of it? Also a lot of these out-of-the-way natural beauties are not so famous now as they obviously deserve to be. A lake would take care of that. A natural arch that has so far been seen by only a few hundred hikers each year would soon be familiar to thousands who would view it from their motorboats. Beauty of nature obviously has to be famous. Otherwise how in the hell will anybody ever explain where he has been?

Two weeks of such recreation are surely more to be wondered at than any week of creation.

If dam building is an illusion deeply rooted in our history and culture, recreation is no more than a blatant commercial fraud, rooted in nothing deeper than the anxieties of a people chronically unsettled and upset by the experience of belonging nowhere. It is a gimmick for selling tents, trailers, stoves, lanterns, sleeping bags, cooking pots, boats, motors, campsites, fishing tackle, gasoline, suntan lotion, bug dope, bad food, hay fever pills, water skis, etc., etc. to people who have no needs that they understand, and who therefore want everything.

The net product of all this wheeling and dealing, this going   *81* to and fro in the earth, is only a well-advertised, countrified, glamorized version of life in a suburb.

And to make the quiet lonely dells and ravines and glades of the Red River country accessible to motorized crowds is quite simply to remove the reasons for going there. People who want to see the beauty of nature from motorboats and automobiles would obviously be just as well pleased, and as fully recreated, at a drive-in movie.

The Gorge, dammed, would be like *Hamlet* rewritten for the feeble-minded. And as illusory—for what is lost is the experience of the living thing itself. Motor vehicles translate the landscape, alter the experience of it, in precisely this way, making possible oversimplifications that are dangerous. A man who has always looked from a motorized perspective will have too comfortable a view of the world; it will seem to him more answerable to his convenience than it is in fact. An artificial lake is a river's oversimplification. A motorboat is an over-simplification of the lake.

I would be among the last, I hope, to discourage anybody from going to the woods. In the name of sanity, let's *all* go, the oftener the better. But let's go without motors. Let's go by rowboat or sailboat or canoe, or on horseback or on skis or on foot. Let's admit that the simple quiet we seek cannot be found with a motor. Motorized, we can only arrive at the uproar we meant to escape.

There are endless ways to amuse oneself and be idle, and most of them lie outside the woods. I assume that when a man
goes to the woods he goes because he needs to. I think he is

drawn to the wilderness much as he is drawn to a woman: it is, in its way, his opposite; it is as far as possible unlike his home or his work or anything he will ever manufacture. For that reason he can take from it a solace—an understanding of himself, of what he needs and what he can do without—such as he can find nowhere else. Though one would surely never want to deny the possibility of being amused, amusement is far from all there is to it. A man drawn to the woods does not go there for what has come to be known as recreation. Why should anything once created need to be re-created? Why should a man, who did not and could not create himself, assume that he can re-create himself? By recreation we mean no such thing, but only distraction from what we ought to be paying attention to: the probable effects of our behavior.

Going to the woods and the wild places has little to do with recreation, and much to do with creation. For the wilderness is the creation in its pure state, its processes unqualified by the doings of people. A man in the woods comes face to face with the creation, of which he must begin to see himself a part—a much less imposing part than he thought. And seeing that the creation survives all wishful preconceptions about it, that it includes him only upon its own sovereign terms, that he is not free except in his proper place in it, then he may begin, perhaps, to take a hand in the creation of himself.

But the Red River Gorge is not now a place of unqualified wilderness. It is not a virgin forest. It has been mined a bit for iron, cut over by loggers, farmed in the few places where the land is not too steep to plow, cut through by roads, and it is surrounded by the mud and garbage machine known as the Affluent Society. To some that makes an argument for destroying the place as it is now, and as it will become if let alone. These people say that if the Gorge is not a *virgin* wilderness then it is not a wilderness, and there is therefore no reason why it should not be flooded and "developed."

One obvious answer is that, because of the depredations of such arguers, Kentucky now has almost no wilderness that is, strictly speaking, virgin. If we want to have a mature forest in which the ecology is unimpaired, then we must realize that we are no longer privileged to have it merely by preserving it. Now, if we want it, we will have to grow it. If we want it we must bow to its conditions, get out of its way, invite it to return.

As long as we insist on relating to it strictly on our own terms—as strange to us or subject to us—the wilderness is alien, threatening, fearful. We have no choice then but to become its exploiters, and to lose, by consequence, our place in it. It is only when, by humility, openness, generosity, courage, we make ourselves able to relate to it on *its* terms that it ceases to be alien. Then it begins to be familiar to us. We begin to see that it is at least partly beneficent. We see that we belong to it, and have our place in it. We see that its terms are the only terms, that in the final sense we have no terms, that our terms are a fiction of our pride.

But if it has become familiar, if we have begun to feel at home in it, that is not because it has become comfortable or predictable or in any way prejudiced in our favor. (It is prejudiced in favor of *life*, leaving it up to us to qualify if we can.) It has not even become less fearful. But the nature of our fear has changed. We no longer fear it as we fear an enemy or as we fear malevolence. Now we fear it as we fear the unknown. Our fear has ceased to be the sort that accompanies hate and contempt and the ignorance that preserves pride; it has begun to be the fear that accompanies awe, that comes with the understanding of our smallness in the presence of wonder, that teaches us to be respectful and careful. And it is a fear that is accompanied by love. We have lost our lives as in our pride we wanted them to be, and have found them as they are—much smaller than we hoped, much shorter, much less important, much less certain, but also more abundant and joyful. We have ceased to think of the world as a piece of merchandise, and have begun to know it as an endless adventure and a blessing.

A man is standing at night in his lighted living room, feeling that in that light he knows himself, that his ends and aims are clear, that his past is coherent and his future certain. And suddenly the roof and the walls are swept away, and he sees that he inhabits a darkness reaching out to the remote lights of the sky. And then he sees that the outer stars also circumscribe a sort of living room, and that beyond them there is a darkness even darker and more immense. All the assumptions based on the premise of his own importance break loose from him. He is like a man stripped of his armor and his arms. He is left naked and humble, brought to earth.

But slowly it dawns on him that his life is a fact, whole and firm, risen up from the ground among other lives. And he feels a blessedness and a joyousness in that. He begins to trust in his own existence. He is a creature among the other creatures, and if the world promises him pain and grief and death, it also promises him health and joy and life. And if he lives generously enough even his suffering and his death may pass back into the world, its increment, to sustain the lives that will follow his. Knowing nothing but what is circumstantial, he begins to live by a sort of faith in circumstance—a faith that his life and the lives of the other creatures all belong together and sustain each other within the life of the creation which is their order and their blessing.

Courage and generosity are the moral conditions of his faith. He must trust himself to the world, freely, openly, without preconditions. He must look upon whatever happens as an opportunity. And he must never exploit his circumstances, for that is to exploit the world and his own life. Then the unity of his life with other lives is broken, the blessedness of the creation is withdrawn, and he is left alone.

A man who loves the world only insofar as it conforms to his expectations (insofar, that is, as he can understand it or use it, as engineers use it) is like an adolescent lover who loves a girl because (he thinks) she loves him. He is encapsuled in himself, and he misses the whole adventure.

A man who loves the world beyond his understanding, welcoming its unexpected blessings and depending on them, in spite of its unexpected trials and dangers, has the wisdom of a man long married to a beloved woman.

I do not believe that the Red River Gorge can be preserved simply by making a law to preserve it. It cannot be preserved simply by defeating the dam builders, for the issue is not, finally, that of the dam. To advocate the preservation of the Gorge is to advocate a profound change in the American mind. It is to go directly against the mentality of economics that has so far been dominant in our national experience, and that has made us unable, as a people, to value any object or any act for itself, but only for its economic worth. We relate to the Red River Gorge not in terms of what it is, but in terms of what it can be marketed for. By this logic everything becomes expendable.

But what appears, on a ledger, to be economic sanity is ecological madness. A man who would value a piece of land strictly according to its economic worth is precisely as crazy, or as evil, as a man who would make a whore of his wife. If we were a civilized people we would not dam the Red River Gorge or overgraze a pasture or strip mine a mountain or pollute a river any more than we would sell our wives and children, because we would understand that the real values of a wilderness or a pasture or a mountain or a river, like the real values of wives and children, are not transferable or trans-formable. They have no monetary equivalents. The Red River Gorge cannot be transformed into a lake and it cannot be replaced by a lake any more than a wife or child can be transformed into or replaced by an insurance payment. In order for the lake to come to be, what is there now must be destroyed. The processes of economics can be reversed: what has been sold can be bought back. But when the laws of economics are applied to the environment, as they have been relentlessly throughout our history, they do not work economically but are irreversibly destructive: all transactions are final. The Red

River Gorge can be destroyed within a length of time and for a price that are calculable and relatively small. The price and the time of its restoration surpass human reckoning. Should our generation destroy the Gorge, and should our grandchildren decide that we were in error, they cannot restore it; at most they can only begin a process of restoration that may take thousands of years.

If we are to preserve anything worth preserving—including, perhaps, our own lives—the economic mentality will have to give way to a mentality that will be ecological. Whereas the economic mentality holds that you give in order to get something commensurate with what you gave, the ecological mentality would center on the awareness that you get—and *far* more than you can ever earn or deserve or understand—in order to give. The nature of the economic mentality is exploitive; its motive is greed. The nature of the ecological mentality would be preserving; its motive would be generosity. That we receive so abundantly as we do from the creation does not merely imply a moral obligation to give, but the giving is the condition of the getting: you can only have, in the fullest sense, what you are prepared to give up; you can only preserve what you have become willing and glad for others to have when you are dead. "Whosoever shall seek to save his life shall lose it; and whosoever shall lose his life shall preserve it." The economic mentality assumes—the message is tirelessly repeated in advertisements and in political praises of affluence—that the blessings of our lives are luxuries and superficialities, ostentations and fashions. The ecological mentality would recognize that in reality the blessings are air and water and

food and sex and warmth and light and darkness and sleep and the lives of other people and other creatures. There is a story of a Zen master who said, "My miracle is that when I feel hungry I eat, and when I feel thirsty I drink." And in the thirty-third psalm it is said that "the earth is full of the goodness of the Lord." We must recover that sense of holiness in the world, and learn to respect and forebear accordingly. Failing that, we have literally everything to lose.

Early in 1968 the state's newspapers were taking note of the discovery, in one of the rock houses in the Gorge, of a crude hut built of short split planks overlaying a framework of poles. The hut was hardly bigger than a pup tent, barely large enough, I would say, to accommodate one man and a small stone fireplace. One of its planks bore the carved name: "D. boon." There was some controversy over whether or not it really was built by Daniel Boone. Perhaps it does not matter. But the news of the discovery and of the controversy over it had given the place a certain fame.

The find interested me, for I never cease to regret the scarcity of knowledge of the first explorations of the continent. Some hint, such as the "Boone hut" might provide, of the experience of the Long Hunters would be invaluable. And so one of my earliest visits to the Gorge included a trip to see the hut.

The head of the trail was not yet marked, but once I found the path leading down through the woods it was clear to me that I had already had numerous predecessors. And I had not gone far before I knew their species: scattered more and more thickly along the trail the nearer I got to the site of the hut was the trash that has come to be more characteristic than shoe-prints of the race that produced (as I am a little encouraged to remember) such a man as D. boon. And when I came to the rock house itself I found the mouth of it entirely closed, from the ground to the overhanging rock some twenty-five feet above, by a chain-link fence. Outside the fence the ground was littered with polaroid negatives, film spools, film boxes, food wrappers, cigarette butts, a paper plate, a coke bottle.

And inside the fence, which I peered through like a prisoner, was the hut, a forlorn relic overpowered by what had been done to protect it from collectors of mementos, who would most likely not even know what it was supposed to remind them of. There it was, perhaps a vital clue to our history and our inheritance, turned into a curio. It reminded me of those little splinters of the true cross that opulent Christians once placed in reliquaries studded with precious stones, thereby making a doodad of their faith. Whether because of the ignorant enthusiasm of souvenir hunters, or because of the strenuous measures necessary to protect it from them, Boone's hut had become a doodad—as had Boone's name, which now stood for a mendacious TV show and a brand of fried chicken. The fore-fatherhood of Boone, who loved the country, is thus overthrown by that of John Swift, who loved money.

I did not go back to that place again, not wanting to be associated with the crowd whose vandalism had been so accurately foreseen and so overwhelmingly thwarted. But I did not forget it either, and the memory of it seems to me to bear, both for the Gorge and for ourselves, a heavy premonition of ruin. For are those who propose damming the Gorge, arguing *convenience*, not the same as these who can go no place, not even a few hundred steps to see the hut of D. boon, without the trash of convenience? Are they not the same who will use the proposed lake as a means of transporting the same trash into every isolated cranny that the shoreline will penetrate? I have a vision (I don't know if it is nightmare or foresight) of a time when our children will go to the Gorge and find there a web-work of paved, heavily littered trails passing through tunnels of steel mesh. When people are so ignorant and destructive that they must be divided by a fence from what is vital to them, whether it is their history or their world, they are imprisoned.

On a cold drizzly day in the middle of October I walk down the side of a badly overgrazed ridge into a deep, steep hollow where there remains the only tiny grove of virgin trees still standing in all the Red River country. It is a journey backward through time, from the freeway droning both directions through 1969, across the old ridge denuded by the agricultural policies and practices of the white man's era, and down into such a woods as the Shawnees knew before they knew white men.

Going down, the sense that it is a virgin place comes over you slowly. First you notice what would be the great difficulty of getting in and out, were it not for such improvements as bridges and stairways in the trail. It is this difficulty that preserved the trees, and that even now gives the hollow a feeling of austerity and remoteness. It feels defiantly set apart like a medieval castle. And then you realize that you are passing among poplars and hemlocks of a startling girth and height, the bark of their trunks deeply grooved and moss-grown. And finally it comes to you where you are; the virginity, the uninterrupted wildness, of the place comes to you in a clear strong dose like the first breath of a wind. Here the world is in its pure state, and such men as have been here have all been here in their pure state, for they have destroyed nothing. It has lived whole into our lifetime out of the ages. Its life is a vivid link between us and Boone and the Long Hunters and their predecessors, the Indians. It stands, brooding upon its continuance, in a strangely moving perfection, from the tops of the immense trees down to the leaves of the partridge berries on the ground. Standing and looking, moving on and looking again, I suddenly realize what is missing from nearly all the Kentucky woodlands I have known: the summit, the grandeur of these old trunks that lead the eyes up through the foliage of the lesser trees toward the sky.

At the foot of the climb, over the stone floor of the hollow, the stream is mottled with the gold leaves of the beeches. The water has taken on a vegetable taste from the leaves steeping in it. It has become a kind of weak tea, infused with the essence of the crown of the forest. By spring the fallen leaves on the stream bed will all have been swept away, and the water, filtered once again through the air and the ground, will take back the clear taste of the rock. I drink the cool brew of the autumn.

And then I wander some more among the trees. There is a thought repeating itself in my mind like an astounded critic: This is a great Work, this is a great Work. It occurs to me that my head has gone to talking religion, that it is going ahead more or less on its own, assenting to the Creation, finding it good, in the spirit of the first chapters of Genesis. For no matter the age or the hour, I am celebrating the morning of the seventh day. I assent to my mind's assent. It *is* a great Work. It is a *great* Work—begun in the beginning, carried on until now, to be carried on, not by such processes as men make or understand, but by "the kind of intelligence that enables grass seed to grow grass; the cherry stone to make cherries."

Here is the place to remember D. boon's hut. Lay aside all questions of its age and ownership—whether or not he built it, he undoubtedly built others like it in similar places. Imagine it in a cave in a cliff overlooking such a place as this. Imagine it separated by several hundred miles from the nearest white men and by two hundred years from the drone, audible even here, of the parkway traffic. Imagine that the great trees surrounding it are part of a virgin wilderness still nearly as large as the continent, vast rich unspoiled distances quietly peopled by scattered Indian tribes, its ways still followed by buffalo and bear and panther and wolf. Imagine a cold gray winter evening, the wind loud in the branches above the protected hollows. Imagine a man dressed in skins coming silently down off the ridge and along the cliff face into the shelter of the rock house. Imagine his silence that is unbroken as he enters, crawling, a small hut that is only a negligible detail among the stone rubble of the cave floor, as unobtrusive there as the nest of an animal or bird, and as he livens the banked embers of a fire on the stone hearth, adding wood, and holds out his chilled hands before the blaze. Imagine him roasting his supper meat on a stick over the fire while the night falls and the darkness   *93* and the wind enclose the hollow. Imagine him sitting on there, miles and months from words, staring into the fire, letting its warmth deepen in him until finally he sleeps. Imagine his sleep.

When I return again it is the middle of December, getting on toward the final shortening, the first lengthening of the days. The year is ending, and my trip too has a conclusive feeling about it. The ends are gathering. The things I have learned about the Gorge, my thoughts and feelings about it, have begun to have a sequence, a pattern. From the start of the morning, because of this sense of the imminence of connections and conclusions, the day has both an excitement and a deep easy comfort about it.

As I drive in I see small lots staked off and a road newly graveled in one of the creek bottoms. And I can hear chain saws running in the vicinity of another development on Tunnel Ridge. This work is being done in anticipation of the lake, but I know that it has been hastened by the publicity surrounding the effort to keep the Gorge unspoiled. I consider the ironic possibility that what I will write for love of it may also contribute to its destruction, enlarging the hearsay of it, bringing in more people to drive the roads and crowd the "points of interest" until they become exactly as interesting as a busy street. And yet I might as well leave the place anonymous, for what I have learned here could be learned from any woods and any free-running river.

I pull off the road near the mouth of a hollow I have not yet been in. The day is warm and overcast, but it seems unlikely to 94 rain. Taking only a notebook and a map, I turn away from the road and start out. The woods closes me in. Within a few minutes I have put the road, and where it came from and is going, out of mind. There comes to be a wonderful friendliness, a sort of sweetness I have not known here before, about this day and this solitary walk—as if, having finally understood this country well enough to accept it on its terms, I am in turn accepted. It is as though, in this year of men's arrival on the moon, I have completed my one-inch journey at last, and have arrived, an exultant traveler, here on the earth.

I come around a big rock in the stream and two grouse flush in the open not ten steps away. I walk on more quietly, full of the sense of ending and beginning. At any moment, I think, the forest may reveal itself to you in a new way. Some intimate insight, that all you have known has been secretly adding up to, may suddenly open into the clear—like a grouse, that one moment seemed only a part of the forest floor, the next moment rising in flight. Also it may not.

Where I am going I have never been before. And since I have no destination that I know, where I am going is always where I am. When I come to good resting places, I rest. I rest whether I am tired or not because the places are good. Each one is an arrival. I am where I have been going. At a narrow place in the stream I sit on one side and prop my feet on the other. For a while I content myself to be a bridge. The water of heaven and earth is flowing beneath me. While I rest a piece of the world's work is continuing here without my help.

Since I was here last the leaves have fallen. The forest has been at work, dying to renew itself, covering the tracks of those of us who were here, burying the paths and the old campsites and the refuse. It is showing us what to hope for. And that we   *95* can hope. And *how* to hope. It will always be a new world, if we will let it be.

The place as it was is gone, and we are gone as we were. We will never be in that place again. Rejoice that it is dead, for having received that death, the place of next year, a new place, is lying potent in the ground like a deep dream.

Somewhere, somewhere behind me that I will not go back to, I have lost my map. At first I am sorry, for on these trips I have always kept it with me. I brood over the thought of it, the map of this place rotting into it along with its leaves and its fallen wood. The image takes hold of me, and I suddenly realize that it is the culmination, the final insight, that I have felt impending all through the day. It is the symbol of what I have learned here, and of the process: the gradual relinquishment of maps, the yielding of knowledge before the new facts and the mysteries of growth and renewal and change. What men know and presume about the earth is part of it, passing always back into it, carried on by it into what they do not know. Even their abuses of it, their diminishments and dooms, belong to it. The tragedy is only ours, who have little time to be here, not the world's whose creation bears triumphantly on and on from the fulfillment of catastrophe to the fulfillment of hepatica blossoms. The thought of the lost map, the map fallen and decaying like a leaf among the leaves, grows in my mind to the force of a cleansing vision. As though freed of a heavy weight, I am light and exultant here in the end and the beginning.

The Photographs

After three and a half years of working in the Red River Gorge, of trying to attain a "true" and meaningful image of its visual experience, I still find myself surprised by its variety. In deep shade or in bright sunlight, there is a tremendous feeling of light and the absence of light—of places to hide or to be fully exposed, bared to all elements. In terms of vision, the Gorge is a place of contrasts, of surprising alternates of light and dark, and this is the way I have tried to show it through my photographs.

GENE MEATYARD

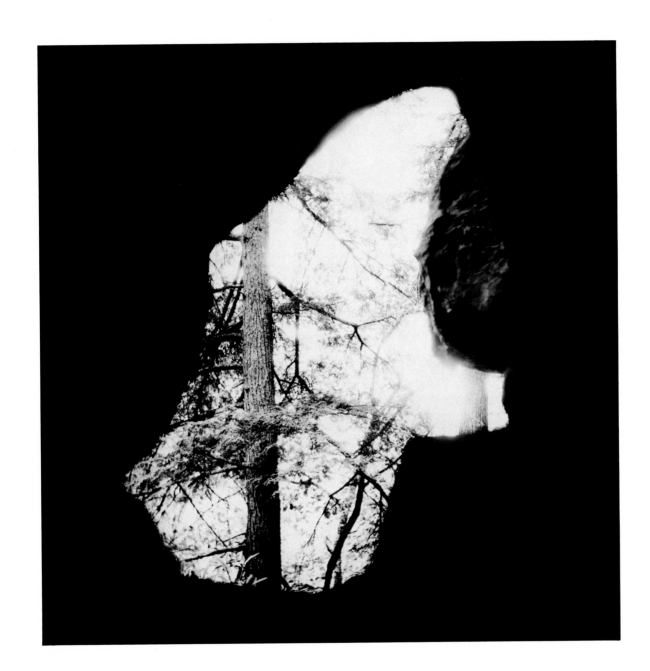